The Lan

A Life and Times of an Ayrshire Farm

c.1500 - 1714

This is a 'labour of love', an escape. I love this land and its history is fascinating with much of it untold, especially the years before 1700. A big thank you to the many people who have listened and helped over the last decade, a special thanks to Diane Baptie, Renee Gillan, Kay McMeekin, Margaret Sanderson, Simon Taylor, and Andrew McInnes. However, all mistakes are own.

This is for Andrew, Alastair, and Iain – my three wonderful boys.

The Lands of Drumfork

A Life and Times of an Ayrshire Farm c.1500 - 1714

Ailsa M. McInnes

carn

Published by
Carn Publishing Ltd.
Lochnoran House,
Auchinleck,
Ayrshire,
KA18 3JW.

First Published in 2024

ISBN - 978 1 911043 25 6

Printed in Great Britain by
Imprint Digital Ltd.,
Upton Pyne, Exeter, Devon, EX5 5HY.

Contents

SETTING THE SCENE

We live in a farm cottage on Drumfork farm near Mauchline, within walking distance of the beautiful Auchinleck Estate, with stunning views over the Ayrshire countryside to Arran in the west and the hills of New Cumnock in the east. ('We' being myself and my husband, also 'into' local history in a big way.) A circular hedged feature at the bottom of the road had always intrigued. There were traces of stonework, possibly something agricultural. Searching old maps online we discovered that it was a well, I then asked the bold question, 'Why would there be a well when there are no people or houses?'

Trying to answer this question and subsequently trying to locate where the old fermtouns had been situated led to research over many years, digging, sometimes literally on the farm, as well as in various archives, books, and online resources. I revisited Latin untouched for over thirty years and learned Secretary Hand to try and decipher sixteenth and seventeenth century documents. Every time we got an answer to something more questions would arise!

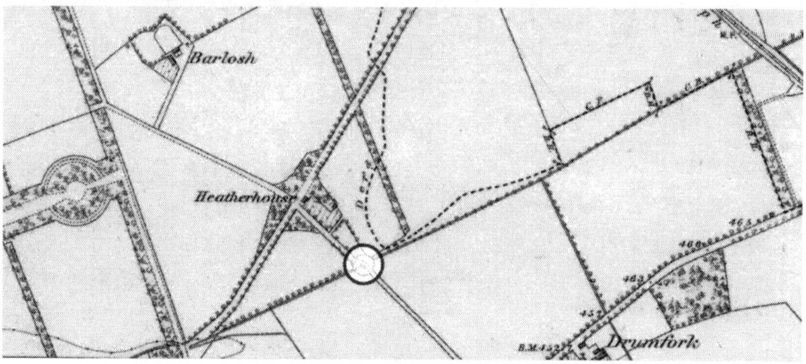

Fig. 1: Heather House

From the 1856 Ordnance Survey Map we found Heather House as well as the outline of two other buildings in the bottom field near the well. Several visits to the National Map Library in Edinburgh ensued, obtaining copies of the first Ordnance Survey maps of Mauchline and the neighbouring parishes and of Roy's map (c.1748) as well as checking out the earlier maps of Ayrshire and Scotland. I found it so frustrating that accurate maps only go back to the mid nineteenth century and that estate maps are so scarce.

The Census returns were searched to find the occupants of Heather House and more about Drumfork and the neighbouring farms. In my naivety I thought about researching all the farms in Meiklewood, the area of Mauchline parish south of the river Ayr. Heather House may formerly have been called Burcuroch cottage as it solely appears in the 1861 Census and the first Ordnance Survey map. A David and Mary Johnstone lived at Burcuroch (of Barlosh) in both the 1841 and 1851 Census of Mauchline parish and by 1861 are living in Heather House which is the only house down from Barlosh. Since no other houses are mentioned and the enumerator would take a similar route it is likely that we are referring to the same building. By the 1871 Census there is no reference to either Burcuroch cottage or Heather House.

However, this led me to google, 'Heather House Auchinleck' and discover a book, *The Correspondence of James Boswell with James Bruce and Andrew Gibb, overseers of the Auchinleck Estate*[1] where I found a reference to Hern Gate, a house on the Auchinleck estate on the road towards

1 Hankins, N. P. & Strawhorn, J. (Editors) *The Correspondence of James Boswell with James Bruce and Andrew Gibb, Overseers of the Auchinleck Estate*

the turnpike at Howford.[2] Could Heather House, a gatehouse on the Auchinleck estate enroute to the Howford Bridge, be a corruption of Hern Gate? Maybe not, but a theory, nonetheless.

'The book', as it is lovingly referred to, was duly purchased and proved to be invaluable. (And yes, costing nearly three figures it is certainly the most expensive book that I own.) From the maps and 'the book' we discovered that what constitutes the modern-day farm of Drumfork originally had a Mains farm as well as several smaller fermtouns; Hern, Ballangape, Gulzie Mailing and Whirr.

Trying to discover more about Drumfork I checked the Index to the Ayrshire Register of Sasines[3] held at the Carnegie Library, Ayr, and that's when I first met Mungo Reid, the earliest known occupant of Drumfork. With his introduction our research took a leap forward as no longer were we researching geographical places but people. People bring history alive. Who were they? What did they do? How did they live? And what was happening in Ayrshire and the wider world? This plunged me into Ayrshire in the sixteenth and seventeenth century, a fascinating world, long gone and very different from ours.

Perhaps not….

---

2 Ibid. p223

3 *Index to the Register of Sasines for Sheriffdom of Ayr and Bailiaries of Kyle, Carrick, and Cunningham 1599-1609, 1617-1634* and *1635-1660.*

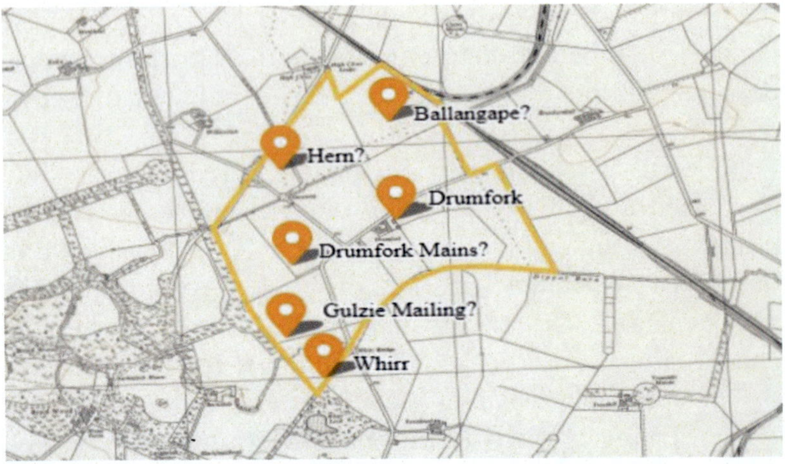

Fig. 2: Fermtouns at Drumfork

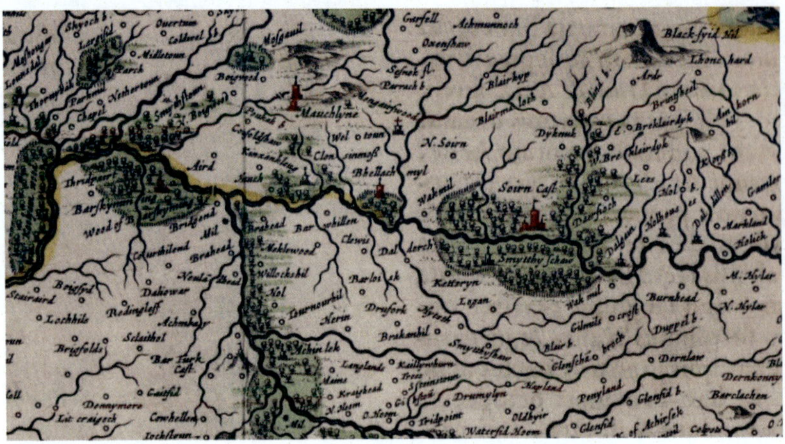

Fig. 3: Blaeu's Map

1

Lands of Drumfork

Modern Drumfork is made up of several smaller fermtouns; Drumfork Mains, Hern, Ballangape, Gulzie Mailing and Whirr, now lost and forgotten apart from Whirr. Imagine how these fermtouns would have looked pre-enclosure without fields, roads, or hedges and with the ancient water courses that still appear after heavy rain. The Dippol burn marks Drumfork's southern boundary as well as Mauchline parish itself and the hollow on the northern edge, the area formerly known as Hern/Ballangape is the northern boundary. The eastern boundary adjoins Brackenhill Farm, now in Sorn parish and the southwestern boundary, at what was Gulzie Mailing and Whirr, abuts the Auchinleck Estate in Auchinleck parish.

The earliest map reference showing Drumfork is Blaeu 1654 (although surveyed in the 1590s) where it is positioned with its neighbours, Brackenhill etc. The earliest recorded name of *Drumfork* in documents is 1555.[1] Drumfork is a Gaelic name, Gaelic being firmly established in Ayrshire by the end of the twelfth century.[2] The first element is Gaelic *druim* 'a ridge', the second is more likely Gaelic *coirce* 'oats', so the modern Gaelic would be *Druim a' Choirce* 'ridge of the

1 Yale University, Beinecke Rare Book and Manuscript Library Boswell Collection GEN MSS 89 Series XV oversize b.129 f.2378

2 Taylor, Simon 'Ayrshire Place-Names: a rich seam still to mine' *Ayrshire Notes* 38 Autumn 2009 p8

Fig. 4: Roy's Map

oats ; oat ridge'.[3] It certainly sits on a ridge and we know from various testaments that oats were grown at Drumfork.

Roy's map of c.1748 shows that there were two Drumforks. Initially this was thought to be an error, however, 'the book' clarified that there were indeed two Drumforks, Drumfork itself and Drumfork Mains.[4] By the eighteenth century the two names were interchangeable, and the 'Mains' had been dropped. In the 1780s and 1790s a Thomas Guthrie farmed Drumfork and a Robert Reid the Mains. The farms were about 100 acres each, substantial for their time, and by

3 Gaelic *ch* (as in *loch*) often appears as *f* in place-names. There is a Drumfork in Alyth parish, Perthshire, with the same meaning. It appears as *Drummacrok* in 1506 (Dunkeld Rental). Simon Taylor pers. comm.
4 Hankins, N. P. & Strawhorn, J. (Editors) *The Correspondence of James Boswell with James Bruce and Andrew Gibb, Overseers of the Auchinleck Estate*, p222

1841 had amalgamated into the one large farm.

The first Ordnance Survey maps show a road leading into a field and this 'road to nowhere' had intrigued. Possibly it was a pathway into the Auchinleck Estate, however, when we searched the parish descriptions in the Ordnance Survey Name Books it was titled an 'occupation road' rather than a 'parish road'.[5] An occupation road must go to somewhere that is occupied - a habitation - and the most likely one is that it was Drumfork Mains. Large foundation boulders are piled up at both sides of this occupation road and its situation fits with Roy's map. If Drumfork had a Mains farm perhaps it was more than just a farm?

If you look closely at the above map, you see the Drumforks and the neighbouring farms which are still there, Brackenhill and Barlosh with Heateth now across the busy A76 but note the farm Piss Wanton. I think someone is having a laugh!

Hern[6] is most likely to be the area at the bottom of the fields near the well. Interestingly, the meaning of Hern as the Scots hirn(e)/hyrn(e) 'a corner, nook, hiding place' fits the landscape very well indeed.[7] The ruins of Heather House/Hern Gate are well hidden in the trees but are still there leading into Hern.

Searching the National Records of Scotland, reference was found to the five-shilling lands of Overmeiklewood being bought in perpetual feu from Melrose Abbey in 1565 by Robert Train (*Trance*) for his mother Agnes Symington (*Symontoun*) who lived there.[8] A brief chronology, in 1575

5 National Map Library Scotland 'Ordnance Survey Name Books'

6 Earliest form *Heirne* alias *Ballengaip* 1602 GD1/186/5

7 Simon Taylor pers. comm. See https://dsl.ac.uk/

8 National Records of Scotland GD1/186/1

a John Train (no doubt a relative of Robert) sold the land to David Reid.[9] A document of 1602 refers to this five-shilling land as *Heirne* alias *Ballengaip.*[10] (It would appear that Overmeiklewood had various pockets of land each with differing valuations, the five-shilling portion being called Hern by 1602.) In 1626 John Reid, David Reid's grandson, sold Hern to Thomas Ferguson, the blacksmith there.[11] John Reid sold the land as he was going to Ireland as part of the Plantation of Ulster, at the same time as kinsman James Reid from Willockshill. When William Ferguson, a descendant of Thomas, died in 1661, he left Hern to his nephew, Alexander Milliken of Duncanziemere (*Duncanziemuir*),[12] and in 1720 it was sold to James Boswell.[13]

The above-mentioned document of 1602 refers to Hern alias Ballangape and they appear to adjoin each other. Ballangape may be in the bottom field where the parish boundary (Sorn disjoined from Mauchline parish in the late seventeenth century) has taken a distinct rectangle round something, possibly a long house, and Ballangape could be a much earlier habitation than Drumfork.

A big puzzle was the meaning of Ballangape.[14] It is a Gaelic name, the first element being Gaelic *baile* 'a farm; homestead', followed by *an* meaning 'of the'. But what is gape or gaip? It may well be from Gaelic *ceap* (Old Gaelic *cepp*). This word has a range of meanings in modern Gaelic including

9 National Records of Scotland GD1/186/3

10 National Records of Scotland GD1/186/5

11 National Records of Scotland GD1/186/8

12 Freepages.rootsweb.com/-alanmilliken/genealogy/Research/Scot-tishRecords/Ayrshire/Mauchline.html

13 National Records of Scotland RS14-7-2-00007

14 Earliest form *Ballingaip* 1555; *Ballangep* 1564

such as 'a block', topographically 'a small lumpy or pointed hill', usually but not always standing on top of a larger hill. Could it possibly apply to Clews Mount? However, as with *cab* it would have to be plural for the *c* to become *g*, so *Baile nan Geap* 'farm of the small, lumpy hills' which does not fit the local landscape. Another meaning of *ceap* is a 'tree-stump', so 'farm of the tree-stumps', perhaps named after it had been recently cleared. In Old Gaelic 'tree-stump' is one the basic meanings of *cepp*. It has been interpreted as such in another 'gap' name in Galloway with Dalnigap (*Dalnagap* 1633) Gaelic *Dail nan Geap* 'haugh of the tree-stumps'.[15] My money is with tree-stumps and harks back to the time when the forest was being cleared. Think Meiklewood.

The location of Guilzie Mailing[16] can be pinpointed accurately from 'the book'. *Mailing* is a rented or tenant-farm (from Scots *mail* 'rent') and *gulzie* or gully is self-explanatory, as the Dippol runs through a rather large gully, and what a beautiful place it is. There is no trace of a dwelling as it has been well ploughed. Some of its land is now part of Drumfork and the remainder part of the Auchinleck Estate. An eighteenth-century tack for Gulzie Mailing has survived giving wonderful descriptions,

> .... 'that the three riggs of crofting in the said farm near opposite the Barnsdale houses'...
> .... 'the short rigg of crofting immediately above the walk end of the yard'....
> ... 'lying upon the head rig running westward towards Affleck's stone dykes'...

15 Simon Taylor pers. comm.

16 Earliest form *Goollymealing* 1713

> ... 'and the ground upon the burns edge over which the Dippol Burn in ordinary spates or floods run'....[17]

Whirr had at least two habitations one of which was still operational up to World War II. A well and strong traces of rig and furrow are evident. It has a magical, peaceful atmosphere with the Dippol running through, although it has been rerouted during nineteenth century drainage work. Whereas the other fermtouns mentioned were part of Drumfork and now lost, it would appear Whirr became part of Drumfork in more recent times, possibly after Drumfork was included in the Auchinleck Estate. Farms do not usually straddle different parishes and Whirr is in Auchinleck parish whereas Drumfork is in Mauchline.

The complexity of place name research can be exemplified by Whirr, which is such an intriguing name. The early forms show that it has completely lost its first element. The earliest form is from a charter of 1564 issued by Mungo Reid (1) for William Reid, which is witnessed by John Livingstone (*Johne Levingstone*) in *Calzequhoir*.[18] It next appears as *Kaillywhurn* in Blaeu's 1654 map of Kyle, then as *Whurr* in Roy's mid eighteenth-century map and *Whirr* in the 1860 Ordnance Survey map.[19] The first element is Gaelic *coille* 'a wood, woodland'. The second element originally began with *ch* since *quh* (also *wh*) is one way in which Scots represents Gaelic *ch*. The final *n* of Blaeu's form – *whurn* must be treated with suspicion, since the map is notorious for typos. If it

17 'Tack of James Boswell for Hugh Pedin, Guilzy Mailing, 1736' Burns Monument Centre, Kilmarnock AA/DC/44/2/2/16
18 Yale University, Beinecke Rare Book and Manuscript Library, Boswell Collection, GEN MSS 89 Series XV oversize b.129 f.2380
19 Ordnance Survey 1860 six-inch first edition Ayr sheet XXXV

were genuine, you would expect a form with *n* to occur again but it does not. The second element is most likely from the Early Gaelic *corr* an adjective meaning 'tapering, cuspidated, peaked pointed, jutting out or up, swelling' or a noun meaning 'rounded and/or tapered point'. This would give *coille chorr* meaning a 'projecting wood'.[20] There are certainly still bends in the Dippol and projections where Whirr is located which would suggest this could be correct.

Drumfork is one small Ayrshire farm, multiply this by all the others, and one begins to realise the amount of local history lost and unrecorded.

20 Thomas Clancy, University of Glasgow pers. comm.

Fig. 5: Mauchline Castle

2

Mauchline Parish; Background

The lands of Drumfork and the people who owned, lived, and worked them make a fascinating history, a microcosm of the history of Ayrshire and indeed Scotland. This is their story.

Mauchline parish was part of a large fertile upland area known as Kylesmure and belonged to Melrose Abbey. The parish was far larger than today as it included Sorn (*Dalgain*) and Muirkirk parishes which did not disjoin until the seventeenth century.

David I (1124 - 1153) and his successors gave vast tracts of land to Anglo-Norman lords who had proved their military worth to stabilise the area and strengthen the central powers of the monarchy. Lands in Ayrshire and Renfrewshire were granted to Walter Fitz Alan to help defend the Clyde and west coast.[1] David also gave generously to the monasteries, including Melrose Abbey. This Cistercian Abbey, founded in 1136 and colonised by monks from Rievaulx Abbey in Yorkshire, was to become one of Scotland's richest abbeys.[2] Walter Fitz Alan granted some of the land of Mauchline parish to Melrose Abbey in 1177[3] and his successors, the Stewarts, continued to add to this. This included the pasture in his forest,

1 Dillon, W. J. *Origins of Feudal Ayrshire*, AANHS Collections, 2nd Series, Vol.3 1955 p67

2 Easson, D. *Medieval Religious Houses in Scotland*, p65

3 Dillon, W. J. *Origins of Feudal Ayrshire*, AANHS Collections, 2nd Series, Vol.3 1955 p68

one plough gate of arable land towards Douglas and a fishery at the mouth of the river Ayr.[4] Those grazing rights, however, did not extend to hunting or hawking.[5] 'Forest' was a legal and recreational term rather than an ecological one, meaning open scrub land and pasture, and not solely woodland.[6] The preservation of game, indeed, the whole economy of the 'Forest' was of huge importance in an age when the time of the freeborn was divided between warfare and the chase.[7]

It is interesting to note the 'perambulation' of Donald and Gilbride as they rode the boundaries of this huge Mauchline parish.[8] They mostly followed the rivers and burns and one can make out some of the route that was taken ... the Rede burn into the burn which flows to the *Duueloch* (Loch Broun now drained) Gaelic 'black loch'... into the *Saxnoc* (Cessnock) to the *Polmulin* ('mill burn' and the mill is on Roy's map) to middle *Acchenebron* (Auchenbrain) to the head of the Need burn to the river Ayr then to the river Lugar and by the source of the Lugar to the *Dufpol* (Dippol) and by the *Dufpol* source out to *Monecapel* (possibly Muirkirk) Gaelic *moine* 'a moss, bog (often a peat bog)' and Gaelic *capali* 'a horse'.[9]

The countryside was largely untouched in twelfth century Scotland and the Cistercians had the capability to improve and expand agriculture, livestock farming and fishing and exploit natural resources such as coal, lead,

4 Innes, Cosmos (editor) *Liber Sancte Marie de Melros*, Vol.1, Bannatyne Club Edinburgh 1837 Nos.66-73 p55-64 referenced as *Liber de Melros*
5 Duncan, A. A. M. *Scotland the Making of the Kingdom*, p422
6 Ibid. p421
7 *Liber de Melros* preface xvi
8 *Liber de Melros* Nos.66-73
9 Simon Taylor pers. comm.

silver, stone, and salt.[10] They were an Order renowned for the taming of marginal lands.[11] Consider the possible meaning of Ballangape and the recently cleared forest. The Cistercians of Melrose Abbey, through the hard graft of their tenants, were able to improve Mauchline parish.

The administrative centre of this large area of Kylesmure was the ecclesiastical grange at Mauchline. Granges were monastic farms which normally included a hall, dormitory, kitchen, barns, and other farm buildings.[12]

The earliest reference to a church in Mauchline is the chapel of St Michael. It is not known whether the Cistercians had taken over an earlier church or whether they had erected it after they had established their grange.[13] In 1315, during the reign of Robert the Bruce, St Michael's chapel became the first parish church for the growing barony of Kyle,[14] and we can assume that this would be Mungo Reid's Church.

In 1430 all the Ayrshire lands belonging to Melrose were created a Barony of Regality meaning that the abbot and monks had almost royal powers over their tenants, excluding the jurisdiction of the King's officers such as the sheriff.[15] About 1450, Abbot Andrew Hunter of Melrose Abbey had the tower built at Mauchline and this was called after him due to the roof boss in the hall which bears his arms.[16] In 1510

10 Hall, Derek *Scottish Monastic Landscapes*, p11

11 Dennison, E Patricia; Gallagher, Dennis; Ewart, Gordon *Historic Mauchline Archaeology and Development*, p4

12 Ibid. p10

13 Easson, D. *Medieval Religious Houses in Scotland*, p81

14 Sanderson, M. H. B. *The Mauchline Account Book of Melrose Abbey 1527-1528*, AANHS 2nd ser. xi (1976) p89

15 Ibid. p88

16 Dennison, E Patricia; Gallagher, Dennis; Ewart, Gordon *Historic Mauchline Archaeology and Development*, p13

Mauchline was created a Burgh with Hunter's Tower, known today as Mauchline Castle, as the administrative headquarters of the abbey's Barony of Kylesmure.[17] By 1521 the Regality was in the hands of Hugh Campbell of Loudoun, Sheriff of Ayr for the king.[18]

In the *Mauchline Account Book of Melrose Abbey* Margaret Sanderson gives a fascinating insight into life in a rural parish in 1528. Kylesmure was 'moorland country' with 'scattered townships' where 'generations of tenant farmers had helped their Cistercian landlords reclaim land' from the forest. 'These kindly tenant farmers enjoyed remarkable security of possession, held their farms for life and enjoyed customary rights of inheritance, the family holding usually passing on death to the nearest heir or kinsman'.[19] Kindly farmers does not describe their nature as it is pronounced kinly!

Within Mauchline Parish the key local families such as Campbell, Reid, Aird, Crawford and Mitchell got on with the business of trying to extract a living from the land and do the best they could for themselves and their kinsfolk.

---

17 Sanderson, M. H. B. *The Mauchline Account Book of Melrose Abbey 1527-1528,* AANHS 2nd ser. xi (1976) p88

18 Ibid. p89

19 Ibid. p88

3

Mungo Reid 1 and the Reids of Kylesmure

Mungo Reid was a tenant of Melrose Abbey. Was he simply a tenant farmer? The feuing of kirklands to sitting tenants during the mid-sixteenth century is well documented, Margaret Sanderson says, 'Moving away from the small feuars who had previously been tenants, we come to proprietors of kirklands among small landed families who had been independently established in Scottish rural society for several generations, but were neither offshoots of the bigger lairds nor cadet branches of noble houses: the Reids and Airds in Kylesmure, feuars of Melrose Abbey.'[1] He was more than a tenant farmer then.

Mungo Reid was born c.1500, a small laird and kindly tenant of Melrose Abbey. Those of his level of society were often referred to by outsiders as 'the gentlemen of Kyle'.[2] His landholding comprised Drumfork, Ballangape and Brackenhill, all the land on the 'ridge'. It is unknown how long his forbears had been at Drumfork, however, as sitting tenants possibly some considerable time. He was married to Mause Crawford (*Craufurd*), most likely the daughter of Hew Crawford (*Craufurd*) in Smiddyshaw, a neighbouring small estate which included Daldorch, and the Crawfords too were tenants of Melrose Abbey. Mause is an unusual name and

1 Sanderson, M. H. B. *Scottish Rural Society in the Sixteenth Century,* p144
2 Sanderson, M. H. B. pers. comm.

appears to be a 'pet' form of Margaret.[3] Or it could be Mary[4] and in a 1564 charter she is referred to as Agnes![5]

The family of Reid was prolific throughout Kylesmure, no doubt all related and connected. John Knox wrote that the enemies of the Reformation tried to set the Reids against the Crawfords, exemplifying the power of the Reids as the Crawfords were 'the most influential tribe, excepting the Campbells, in that district during the sixteenth century.'[6] The earliest reference to the Reids can be traced back to William Reid (*Rede*) of Barskimming, who obtained a Charter for Barskimming from Robert II dated 12th October 1377.[7] Or 'William Rede, son of John Rede, was granted a Charter of the lands of Barskimming, Ayrshire 12th October 1375'.[8] You can take your choice between Paterson and Burke. James Rollie says that the 'Reids of Barskimming were a family of some prominence but the other Reid families of Merkland, Daldilling and later Ballochmyle may not have been of the same standard.'[9] John Knox had suggested that a 'combination of interests among the surname, their territories would have taken the form of a belt around Kyle roughly following the course of the river Ayr from Trabboch in the west through Barskimming and Ballochmyle and out toward the moorland

3 Anderson, John 'Calendar of the Laing Charters AD 854-1830' belonging to the University of Edinburgh No.2048 dated March 1630 mentions a Margaret alias Mausye Mitchell. Referenced as 'The Laing Charters'
4 *Dictionaries of the Scots Language*::SND::0089370 (dsl.ac.uk)
5 Yale University, Beinecke Rare Book and Manuscript Library Boswell Collection GEN MSS 89 Series XV oversize b.129 f.2380
6 Paterson, James *History of the County of Ayr*, vol.2 p335
7 Ibid. p439
8 Dewar, Peter Beauclerk (Editor) *Burke's Landed Gentry of Great Britain, The Kingdom in Scotland*, p 1155
9 Rollie, James *The Invasion of Ayrshire*, p60

parish in the south where the Daldilling family lived.'[10] Indeed, the Reids were at the aforementioned places as well as Drumfork and other areas of this huge Mauchline parish. The Clan Campbell Abstracts shows Reids in over fifty distinct fermtouns in the first half of the seventeenth century.[11] The Reids grew in prominence and gained land during the sixteenth century only to lose it in the seventeenth century. Whereas Ballochmyle and Barskimming would become well known estates in the eighteenth and nineteenth centuries, albeit without Reids, Drumfork and Daldilling would revert to being 'merely' farms. Unfortunately, this widespread family rarely seem to feature in local history accounts many of which do not venture further back than 1700.

We know that Mungo Reid of Drumfork was closely related to the Barskimming Reids as in 1577 he was curator to John Reid. 'John Reid of Barskimming, on the 21st September with his awin hand, with advis and consent of Mungo Reid of Drumfork, William Reid of Makestoun and David Reid in Thirdpart (*Thridpart*), his curators.'[12] The above Reid men are probably great uncles of this John Reid of Barskimming. Mungo, William, and David are family names and the Christian names for Mungo of Drumfork's sons. There was a Makestoun and a Thirdpart close to Barskimming and it is likely that they are the ones being referred to, although there was another Makestoun east of Trabboch and a Thirdpart south of Drumfork.[13]

10 Ibid. p60

11 Paton, Henry (Editor) *The Clan Campbell Abstracts Vol.5 Entries relating to Campbells in the early unprinted records relating to Ayrshire 1515-1650*

12 Paterson, James *History of the County of Ayr,* Vol.2 p439

13 Blaeu *Coila Provincia 1654,* National Library of Scotland

Barskimming today has its grand nineteenth century mansion but there would have been a tower house there in the sixteenth century and beyond, strategically protected on two sides by the river Ayr. John Reid of Barskimming was a descendant (possibly great grandson) of Adam Reid, one of the 'Lollards of Kyle.' This was a group of thirty people, one of the most notable being this Adam Reid of Barskimming, brought before James IV in 1494 by Archbishop Blackadder of Glasgow on a charge of heresy. They were acquitted as Adam Reid managed to talk his way out of a tricky and potentially serious situation.[14] Sanderson comments that 'Religious dissent was a marked feature of some Ayrshire families in the first half of the sixteenth century.'[15] Although Lollardy was not co-ordinated and its followers interpreted the Bible in various ways, it enabled them to question ideas and bring credence to the idea of reform from outside the Catholic Church. Margaret Aston says that 'Lollards may not actually make Protestants but they could sow fertile seeds of doubt.'[16]

Adam Reid was known to James IV, and four years later in 1498 was granted land in Ardcarden in Kintyre for his military service in putting down a rebellion by the 'men of the isles.'[17] Airds Castle, also known as Ardcarden, of strategic importance in controlling the Kilbrannan Sound between Kintyre and Arran, came into the possession of the Crown following the forfeiture of John, Lord of the Isles.[18] As well as gaining Ardcarden and adjoining land, Adam Reid

14 Sanderson M. H. B. *Ayrshire and the Reformation,* p40

15 Ibid. p46

16 Ibid. p46

17 Rollie, James *The Invasion of Ayrshire,* p62

18 Historic Environment Scotland, Scheduled Monument 3177, Airds Castle.

was to maintain six archers for the King's service against the inhabitants of the Western Isles.[19] Men in this echelon of society were either at war or honing their martial skills by hunting. This is a local example of late fifteenth century warfare and James IV's campaigns against the powerful Lord of the Isles. Adam Reid would take his Barskimming retainers with him to battle. Would his other Ayrshire kin join him, those of the family possibly in Drumfork, Daldilling and elsewhere?

We have an earlier reference to Adam Reid and Brackenhill, the neighbouring land to Drumfork, from the records of the Parliament of Scotland.[20] In July 1490, Thomas and Catherine Johnson brought an action to the Parliament complaining that George Campbell, Sheriff of Ayr, Adam Reid and James of Douglas had destroyed their tack and smallholding at Brackenhill, spoiling six 'days' worth' of hay, laying waste the house and destroying the corn and goods. This is a fascinating snapshot of the time featuring three of the most important men of the area and, no doubt, their entourage of horsemen. Perhaps they would have ridden across Drumfork too. Possibly it was a dispute as to who owned the tack and the Sheriff of Ayr thought he could remove the Johnsons by force. It was brave of the Johnsons to take their case to the parliament but as they had lost everything, how were they to survive. They won their case and received twenty shillings compensation, a substantial amount in 1490. An interesting point is that ten witnesses were each to receive five shillings. Unfortunately, their names are not included as perhaps they

19 Dewar, Peter Beauclerk (Editor) *Burke's Landed Gentry of Great Britain, The Kingdom in Scotland,* p 1155

20 *Records of the Parliament of Scotland* 1491/4/40 NAS PA2/6, 1st part, f.29r-v

Fig. 6: Linlithgow Palace

would have mentioned the Reids and other tenants who were at Drumfork and Ballangape. Arthur Duncan was the tenant of Brackenhill, receiving his tack from Melrose Abbey, so the Johnsons were possibly his subtenants. Note the name Johnson and remember who lived at Heather House nearly four hundred years later.

We are beginning to see the rather wild Ayrshire that Mungo and his close relations inhabited. Some records survive to give a tantalising glimpse of this world.

In January 1526 Mungo rode out with other Ayrshire gentry, including his Crawford father-in-law and brothers-in-law, to the first battle of Linlithgow Bridge.[21] Although the first battle of Linlithgow Bridge is referred to as a battle, no actual fighting took place. It was part of the machinations

21 *Register of the Privy Seal of Scotland,* Vol.4 No.1540 p.248

of the Scottish nobility to wrest the minor James V from the control of his stepfather, Archibald Douglas, 6th Earl of Angus. Angus had organised that a council of noblemen should look after James V for three months at a time on a rota basis, Angus naturally being first. However, when the time came to hand him over Angus refused and James V remained a virtual prisoner at Edinburgh Castle. Queen Margaret accused Angus of treason and Angus got the king to write a letter stating that he was a 'willing guest of the Douglas'. Other correspondence was smuggled out refuting this and calling on his mother to come and save him, with an army if need be. Queen Margaret (formerly Margaret Tudor widow of James IV and estranged wife of Archibald Douglas) and her new ally the Earl of Moray marched south with 600 followers, meeting the Earl of Arran and his forces at Linlithgow, planning to march on to Edinburgh together. Arran had about 5000 men including the Ayrshire contingent mentioned in the remission of 1551/2 which included 'our' Mungo. However, Angus placed the king at the head of the Edinburgh militia and along with Lennox and Argyll and some 7000 troops marched to Linlithgow. Arran decided that it might not be wise to take up arms against the king and fled, his army dispersed, and the Ayrshire men rode home again.[22] Whether Mungo was involved in the subsequent battle of Linlithgow Bridge in September 1526 is unknown. Frustration!

The following year, 1527, as part of an ongoing feud the Earl of Cassillis was murdered near Prestwick by a large group of Campbell of Loudoun's men. Hew Crawford in Smiddyshaw, father-in-law to Mungo, is cited on suspicion of being concerned in this murder, as is George Reid in

22 Battle of Linlithgow Bridge www.bolb.org.uk

Fig. 7: Repair after the siege of Tantallon Castle, 1528

Daldilling, again close kin to Mungo. Is Mungo Reid one of this contingent as Pitcairn refers to another hundred unnamed men? This is Pitcairn as in Pitcairn's Criminal Trials, a good read if you're bored some evening. Gory stuff![23] You can imagine this huge band of men lying in wait at Prestwick dunes for the Earl and his party to ride by, just another few miles and they would have reached safety.

It appears that the Ayrshire men were active again at the Siege of Tantallon castle in October 1528.[24] By this time James V had escaped the Earl of Angus's custody and had laid siege to the castle. James V rewarded Hew Crawford of Smiddyshaw, Mungo's father- in- law, with the goods 'both moveable and unmoveable of Patrick Campbell of Lanemark'.

23 Pitcairn, Robert *Ancient Criminal Trials in Scotland,* Vol.1 p36

24 *Register of the Privy Seal* Vol.1 No.4010 p582

They had been confiscated by the king as Patrick Campbell had not joined the army that had 'passed enroute' to the siege of Tantallon. Hew Crawford would have had to go and seize Campbell of Lanemark's goods himself which would no doubt involve a bit of a fight! Unquestionably, Patrick Campbell was not at the siege, and although we do not know for certain if Hew Crawford was, this would seem highly likely, and he had certainly found favour with the king. This would also imply that many Ayrshire men joined the king's army, possibly 'our' Mungo?

These three examples, Linlithgow, the murder of Cassillis and the siege of Tantallon show the warlike period of sixteenth century Ayrshire and for every lord/laird that went to war there would be an estimated 10 followers – tenants, cottars, and servants.[25]

This was, of course, a time of bloodfeud, one of the most famous and well documented being between the Cunninghams of Glencairn and the Montgomerys of Eglinton in what is now North Ayrshire.[26] We automatically think of the Borders and the 'Border Reivers' as a place of raiding and feuding, but Ayrshire seems to have been a lawless place too. From a charter of 1574 we know that the Green in the north of Mauchline had the butts for archery practice[27] and the King and parliament regularly enforced by statute the practice of shooting with a bow and arrow. In every parish the young men turned out for archery practice and 'wappenschaws' (exhibition of arms) and in many places archery practice was held every Sunday after the Church service.[28] The kirk at

25 Fergusson, Sir James *The Ayrshire Casualties at Pinkie*, p37

26 Brown, Keith M., *Bloodfeud in Scotland 1573-1625*, p85

27 Melrose Regality Records p260

28 Hay, J., *History of Kilwinning*, p52

Stobo, near Peebles, has grooves in the stonework reputedly by arrows being sharpened.

In 1555 Mungo received his Charter from Melrose Abbey and is no longer a tenant but holds his land in perpetual feu.[29] He is now described in documents as Mungo Reid of Drumfork rather than in Drumfork. The Commendator, James Stewart, the new style lay head of the monastic corporation had made a feu contract with the Kylesmure tenants on 4th May 1555.[30] 'Previously in 1532, Pope Clement had issued a papal dispensation to allow James V to tax the church, initially to pay for a College of Justice. However, this was merely a pretext for the wholesale raising of revenue to finance royal expenditure and although wealthy the Church was forced to sell the rights to ever increasing areas of land. Forbidden by canon law to sell its land, this process of feuing meant the Church was still the nominal owner of the land but since the feu was held in perpetuity, it was the sale of land in everything but name. Fifty percent of Church feus went to sitting tenants and the other fifty to new landowners who could then charge higher rents than the Church had.'[31] We have evidence that Mungo was in Drumfork in 1526[32] but do not know when he acquired Brackenhill, certainly Arthur Duncan was the tenant of Melrose in 1490.[33] There were Bells

29 Yale University, Beinecke Rare Book and Manuscript Library Boswell Collection GEN MSS 89 Series XV b.113, f 2049 Papal confirmation, charter, and sasine for Mungo Reid

30 National Records of Scotland GD150/1455

31 Haggart, Craig *The late medieval Church; the rise of Protestantism and Catholic reform, Scotland under the Stewart kings 1371-1603* p6-7

32 *Register of the Privy Seal of Scotland* Vol.4 No.1540 p.248

33 *Records of the Parliament of Scotland* 1491/4/40 NAS PA2/6, 1st part, f.29r-v

in Ballochmyle in 1557[34] but within twenty years replaced by the Reids of Ballochmyle, John Reid father of Moses and Hugh, close kin to Mungo.[35] Possibly the Reids had the wealth to buy up church land at this time.

Receiving a feu charter involved a considerable financial outlay for these individual tenants, including a down-payment, an increase in their annual dues and some periodic payments.

Frustratingly, Mungo's Charter for Drumfork is at Yale University and too fragile to be copied. (Mungo Reid's charter box ultimately ended up with the Boswell Papers which were purchased by Yale University.) There are more accessible charters for this period and the Drumfork Charter would probably follow a similar format.[36] Annual dues included 'arriage and carriage', when a certain number of day's use of horses was given to Melrose, and 'bondage silver' which appears to be the number of days work at harvest time commuted to a monetary sum. The charters also specified which mill was to be used and that the tenants were to help with the upkeep of the mill and the place at Mauchline, one assumes this is Mauchline castle or Mauchline Mains itself. They were required to ride out and aid the monastery in times of war and Melrose was still entitled to take the natural resources like wood and stone from the lands. If they failed to pay their feu ferme for three consecutive terms or if they conspired against the monastery, then everything would become null and void. However, the land that had possibly been in Mungo's family for generations is now his.

---

34 Melrose Regality Records p154-55

35 Ibid. p269

36 Laing Charters No.642, 643, 668 p167 & p173

Fortunately, the feu charter for Mungo Reid was eventually forthcoming from Yale University.[37] The oversize copy was obtained and although fragile and faded it is tremendous to know that Mungo Reid touched this parchment. It along with other documents survived in his charter box and almost 500 years on we can read them online.

One of the most exciting discoveries from this 1555 Melrose charter is that Mungo was a wealthier tenant than first envisaged as his feu charter is for the three-pound six shilling and nine penny land of Drumfork, Ballangape and Brackenhill as well as the seven merks and one penny land of Glenbuck Eister. He is a laird, therefore, of about four hundred acres. The baillies for granting sasine were Robert and Mungo (*Kentigern*) Crawford, his wife's brothers, demonstrating the close ties of kinship between the two families.[38] The charter is very fragile and difficult to translate, a 1564 charter[39] repeats much of the original, 'the lands are held from the monastery of Melrose in feu and heritage forever with all the rights ancient and devised boundaries in length and breadth in houses, buildings, woods, plains, moors, marches, ways, paths, waters, pools, streams, meadows, grazings and pastures, mills, multures and their sequels, hawkings, huntings, fishings, petaries, turbaries, coals, coal-heughs, rabbits, warrens, doves, dovecots, apples, apple presses, brass -foundries, brewhouses, woods, groves, thickets, timber, logs, quarries, stone and lime and common pasture, with free entry and exit, with all and whole their liberties, commodities, profits, easements and

37 Yale University, Beinecke Rare Book and Manuscript Library Boswell Collection GEN MSS 89 Series XV oversize b.129 f.2378

38 Thank you to Eila Williamson for transcribing this part of the charter

39 Yale University, Beinecke Rare Book and Manuscript Library Boswell Collection GEN MSS 89 Series XV oversize b.129 f.2380

pertinents, both named and unnamed, below and above the earth, near and far, belonging to the lands or which shall happen to belong to them in future, freely, quietly, fully, wholly, honourably, well and in peace without any revocation, contradiction or obstacle.' Every eventuality seems to be covered. And, unlike the charters described above, Melrose does not appear to have entitlement to any resources of the land. The annual feu payment was nine merks three shillings and two pennies in two instalments at Pentecost and St Martin's.

From the Melrose Regality Records, we learn that Drumfork used the mill at Catrine. A Precept of Clare Constat[40] of 1577 shows that a Moses Reid, as heir to his brother Hugh Reid, (and we will see this Hugh Reid in Netherfield of Ballochmyle witnessing several charters with Mungo Reid of Drumfork) was to have half the multures and his brother, John Reid of Ballochmyle younger, the other half. The other farms required to use Catrine Mill were Bruntshield, Daldilling, Holehouse, Burnhead, Dalgain, Gilmilnscroft, Logan, Heateth, Brackenhill, Glenshamrock, Lindsay Hill, Clewes, Whiteflat, Catrine, Montgarswood, Ballochmyle, Blackside, Smiddyshaw, Daldorch, Blindburn and Roundshaw.[41] A charter of 1634 for John Reid younger of Ballochmyle (most likely the son of the John above) lists the same farms.[42] However, by this date George Reid of Daldilling

40 Melrose Regality Records p269

41 Names in their original form *Brentschield, Daldilling, Hoilhous, Burneheid, Dalgane, Gilmiliscroft, Logane, Heateth, Brakinhill, Glenshamerok, Lindesayis Hill, Clewis, Quheitslat, Chatherin, Montgarswode, Ballochmylln, Blaksyd, Smiddieschaw, Daldrocht, Blindburne, Roundschaw.*

42 *Register of the Great Seal* Vol.9 no.91 p40

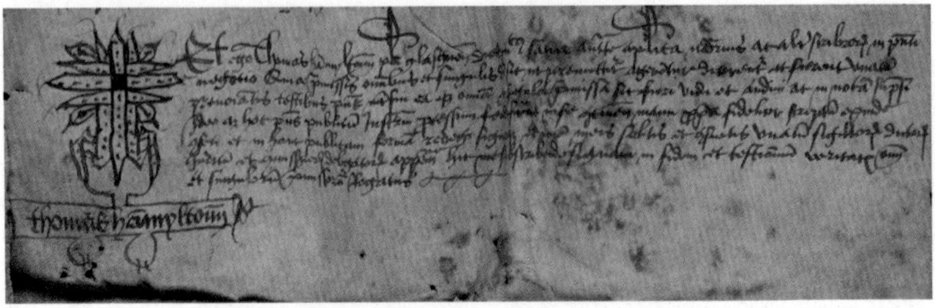

Fig. 8: Thomas Hamilton's signature

has the other half of the multures for Catrine Mill.[43] When did Ballochmyle cease to be a working mill, if it ever was one, as Catrine is being used in the sixteenth century? Or is it the same mill known by different names in different time periods?

In 1556 there was Confirmation by the Papal Delegate of this Charter for Mungo Reid and happily the outsize charter can be obtained.[44] This is a fantastic charter of seven pages of tight knit Latin. However, the elaborate signature of the notary for the diocese of Glasgow, Thomas Hamilton (*Hamyltoun*), is not to be missed.

Within four years of this Papal Confirmation Scotland was a protestant country. What were Mungo and the other Reids' contribution and attitude to this? The Reids' Lollard background has already been mentioned. We know that the Ayrshire gentry were heavily involved in pro Protestant activities, e.g., George Wishart was turned away from Mauchline Church in 1544 by Campbell of Loudoun and preached at Mauchline Moor instead.[45] Mungo was

43 *Register of the Great Seal* Vol.9 no.93 p42

44 Yale University, Beinecke Rare Book and Manuscript Library Boswell Collection GEN MSS 89 Series XV oversize b.129 f.2379

45 Dennison, E Patricia; Gallagher, Dennis; Ewart, Gordon *Historic Mauchline Archaeology and Development*, p20

friends with Robert Campbell of Kingencleugh, a staunch supporter of reform, evidence of this friendship includes Mungo witnessing Charters as well as the close proximity of Drumfork and Kingencleugh. John Knox preached locally and often visited Kingencleugh, being a great friend of Robert Campbell.[46] Knox's second wife was a 'local girl', Margaret Stewart of Ochiltree, daughter of Andrew Stewart, second Lord Ochiltree. In 1562 many of the Ayrshire gentry signed the 'Band of Ayr'. Knox lists the notable persons and mentions that another hundred people had signed.[47] Perhaps Mungo Reid was one of this hundred? According to Rollie, 'Ayrshire had obtained something of a radical image during the Wars of Independence when the 'lesser barons' had provided a solid backbone of support to both Wallace and Bruce when the more powerful and established amongst the nobility had deserted the cause.'[48] In Ayrshire there was 'a more independent type of laird who could more easily pursue personal convictions without fear of punishment or rebuke from a local superior.'[49]

People usually have some idea of life in sixteenth century Scotland when they think of Mary Queen of Scots. When she visited Ayrshire in 1563, Sir Matthew Campbell of Loudoun, sheriff of Ayr, welcomed her to Ayr and the local gentry would have been presented to her.[50] It was violent times with the nobility fighting and plotting, carving up power and wealth for themselves and their families. Apart from the violence, has much really changed with those in power today?

46 Paterson, James *History of the County of Ayr*, p332

47 Knox, John *History of the Reformation*, p56

48 Rollie, James *The Invasion of Ayrshire*, p63

49 Ibid. p65

50 southayrshirehistory.wordpress.com/page/7/ The 1563 visit to Ayrshire of Mary Queen of Scots

In 1564 there was a Charter by Mungo for his eldest son William Reid.[51] Again, access is available to the oversize document.[52] It throws up more questions than answers! This charter is for the sale of the lands of Drumfork, Brackenhill, Ballangape and Glenbuck Eister from Mungo Reid to his son and heir apparent, William. Why on earth would he and 'others' be buying the land that he was due to inherit? Possibly Mungo was struggling financially, and it was a way for William to make sure he gained his inheritance. The Charter does not indicate who the 'others' are but it was drawn up shortly before William's marriage to Isabel Mure of Park. Would her father and grandfather be putting up money to secure her future husband's inheritance? However, Mungo was to have the free liferent of the lands. Intriguingly it also mentions the third land which had been formerly granted to his wife Agnes Crawford. Could Glenbuck Eister be hers? And why is she Agnes when her testament of 1572 clearly uses the name Mause? The witnesses are named as Adam Reid in Drumfork, possibly William's brother, William Richardson (*Rechertson*) in Ballangape and John Livingstone (*Johne Levingstone*) in Whirr (*Calzequhoir*).

Glenbuck Eister is no more as Glenbuck House was built on its lands in 1879 by Charles Howatson, the local landowner.[53] It too has gone with only traces of the garden still in existence. Also, when Mungo Reid owned Glenbuck Eister there would have been no loch, just bog. The loch was only created in 1802 by James Finlay for his Catrine Cotton

51 Yale University, Beinecke Rare Book and Manuscript Library Boswell Collection GEN MSS 89 Series XV b.113, f 2049 Papal confirmation, charter, and sasine for Mungo Reid

52 Ibid. oversize b.129 f.2380

53 Love, Dane *The River Ayr Way*, p15

Works.[54]

Whatever financial problems Mungo had by 1575, as previously mentioned, Hern was purchased for his second son, David.[55] Mungo was in the ascendancy and consolidating his landholding. He appears to be well connected to local lairds, Wallace of Shewalton and Lynn of Bourtreehill, witnesses to William Reid's testament, more of which shortly, and also part of the Ayrshire contingent at Linlithgow Bridge. Lynn of Bourtreehill is a fascinating history, the land is now an Irvine housing scheme but still includes the remnants of the original castle and later mansion.[56]

Mungo Reid witnessed several documents and charters giving insight into his peer group, the wider family relationships, various land holdings, and occasionally some tenants' names.

The main sources are documents from the National Records of Scotland, the Laing Charters, and the Melrose Regality Records. If only more had survived it would have helped build a better picture of Kylesmure landholdings.

On 1st June 1562 at Kingencleugh, Mungo witnesses a charter re a marriage between John Crawford and Janet Durie. John is the eldest son of Robert Crawford of Smiddyshaw (and possibly Mungo's nephew.) Janet is the daughter of Elizabeth Campbell in Tordnis. It appears that Janet is under twenty-one as she has curators, Robert Campbell of Kingencleugh and James Mitchell of Burnhead. The lands mentioned and their values are Smiddyshaw and Daldorch 25s 4d, Heateth 46s, Redrae (*Reidwrayth* also known as *Clerkscheillis*) in

54 Ibid. p13

55 National Records of Scotland GD1/186/3

56 Morton, A. J., *An Independent Review of the History and Surface Archaeology of a forgotten Medieval Estate*, PE 1209/D

Barmure 28s. Other witnesses include Robert Campbell of Kingencleugh, his brother George Campbell, Robert Mitchell of Braehead (*Brayheid*) and William Allan in Mauchline.[57]

On 25th November 1567 Mungo witnesses a sasine of the lands of Greenockton referring to an earlier charter of 1565. Other witnesses include Robert Crawford of Smiddyshaw, his son John Crawford (mentioned in above marriage charter?) and Robert Reid of Bruntshield.[58]

The 1565 charter to which the above refers mentions Hugh Crawford, son of the late Hugh Crawford in Drumdow. The lands of Greenockton are valued at 10s and occupied by John Lekprevick and the lands of Netherwood are valued at 5s and occupied by Matthew Arkill.[59]

The above charter shows the close relationship between the Crawfords of Smiddyshaw and the Crawfords in Drumdow.

On 30th May 1571 Mungo witnesses a sasine granting Matthew Reid the 10s land of Barwheys (*Barquhois*) which was occupied by Robert Wilson. Matthew Reid was the son of the deceased Robert Reid of Bruntshield. Barwheys had been in the hands of John Reid, Robert's brother, and John was to continue to have the liferent of Barwheys. Other witnesses include Hugh Reid in Ballochmyle, Robert Wilson in Barwheys and James Reid, Matthew's brother.[60] There is a close relationship between Mungo Reid of Drumfork and Robert Reid of Bruntshield/Merkland, not only in witnessing charters, but in similar naming patterns. The Merkland Reids appear to be the only other family using the Christian name

57 Melrose Regality Records p318

58 Laing Charters No.830 p209

59 Laing Charters No.792 p200

60 National Records of Scotland RH6/2219

Mungo.

A week later, 8th June 1571 at Netherfield, (probably where Ballochmyle Golf Course is now situated) Mungo witnessed a charter of sale for the above land by Sir John Reid, brother of deceased Robert Reid of Bruntshield, to his friend Matthew Reid, lawful son of Robert Reid, the 10s land of Barwheys occupied by Robert Wilson. Other witnesses were brothers James and William Reid.[61] Is this the same Sir John Reid, minister at Auchinleck, who will be mentioned further?

Did these local worthies meet up to clear the legal paperwork, or were they already getting together for something else and did the paperwork while they were together, as the next charter was witnessed on the same day at Netherfield? And we should not forget the role of the clerk in writing up all these charters, sasines and testaments. They too had to practice. Overleaf is an illustration of a clerk 'doodling' to get just the right effect for Mungo (*Quentigern*) Reid.[62]

On 8th June 1571 at Netherfield Mungo witnessed a charter for the 20d land of Welton (*Voulton*) occupied by John Adam. John Reid, brother of deceased Robert Reid of Bruntshield, was granting this to William Reid, brother of John Reid of Ballochmyle, other witnesses were the brothers James and Mathew Reid.[63]

There was no standardisation of spelling, people and place names can be different, even in the same document. The values given to land had been decided during the reign of Alexander III. By the sixteenth century the monetary value far exceeded this, but it was an accurate way of knowing

61 National Records of Scotland RH6/2223

62 National Records of Scotland CC9/7/37/1

63 Melrose Regality Records p246

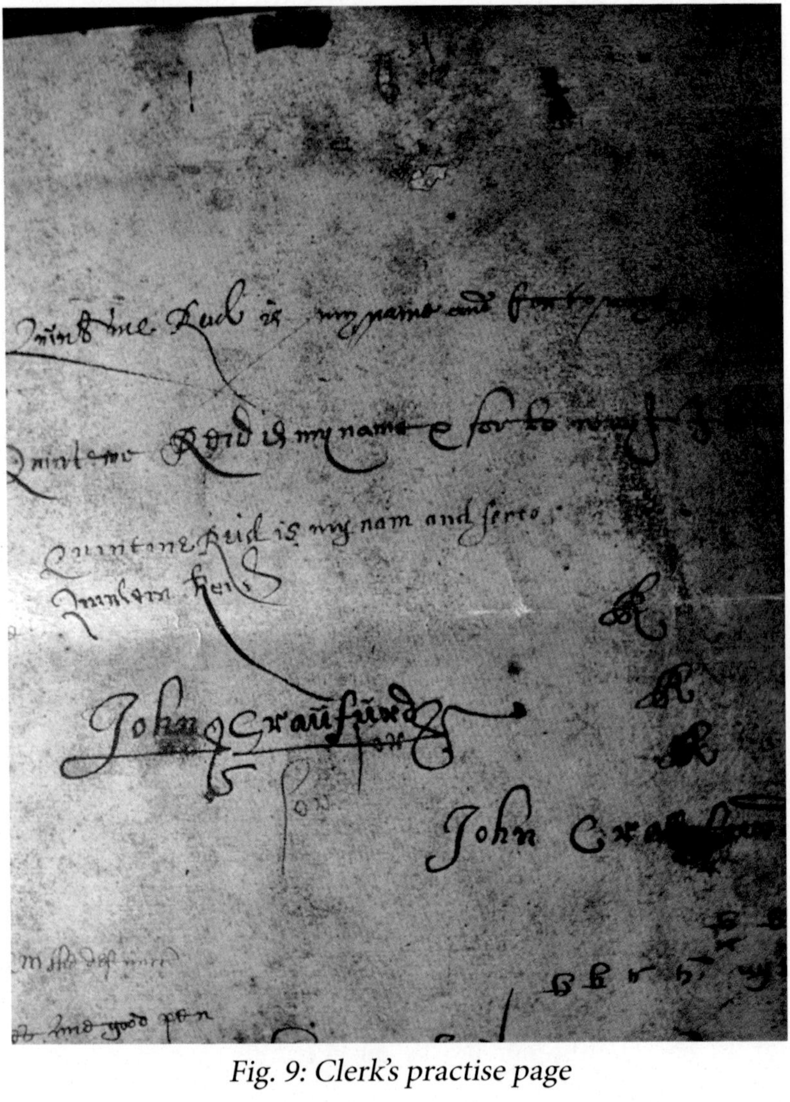

Fig. 9: Clerk's practise page

which parcel of land was being referred to. The value of old extent and the name of the person occupying the land usually sufficed. (No GPS in the sixteenth century.)

On 19th June 1574 Mungo again witnesses a charter by Thomas Reid for the 30d lands of Greenockton occupied by James Reid in Wellwood and the 7d lands of Grassyards occupied by Margaret Hamilton and others not identified. Thomas Reid is the son of the deceased Gilbert Reid in Wellwood. Other witnesses were Hugh Reid in Netherfield and William Reid in Redrae.[64]

On 13th July 1575 at Nether Templand, Mungo was not witnessing a charter, but was mentioned in one. This is the charter for Hern. Robert Train granted the 5-shilling land of Overmeiklewood occupied by John Veddell to David Reid, son of Mungo Reid of Drumfork. Witnesses were Hugh Reid in Netherfield and William Reid in Mauchline.[65] The same charter is recorded in the National Records of Scotland, mentioning that David is Mungo's second son and that Veddell would today be Waddell.[66]

Although Mungo lived to a good age there must have been great sadness in 1572 when William Reid, his eldest son and heir apparent, became ill and aware that death was imminent dictated his testament to Mungo, although for some reason this was not registered until 1646![67] As Mungo Reid (4) was sinking deeper into debt in the mid-1640s there was a lot of legal paperwork, and this testament was possibly included with this. It's rather moving, William Reid, 'being sick and infirm, visited by the hand of God, yet nevertheless

64 Melrose Regality Records p272

65 Melrose Regality Records p262

66 National Records of Scotland GD1/186/3

67 National Records of Scotland CC9/7/30

ripe in mind'. He appointed his wife Isobel Mure and his youngest son Adam Reid as executors with his 'gudes and gear' and appointed his father Mungo Reid and his father-in-law John Mure of Park tutors and overseers of his children. It is interesting to note what is included in the inventory from this Testament, the oats and barley, his cattle and his horses and mares as well as his plenishings and gear. No one appeared to owe him money, but there was a substantial number of people to whom he owed money, which is not unusual in pre-banking days, everybody seemed to owe somebody money. And note the family relationships, he leaves his brother David £6/13/4 once his debts have been paid and his daughter Agnes his remaining goods. His youngest son, Adam, is to receive 100 merks when Mungo, his eldest son and heir, marries. Witnesses at Shewalton on the 8th May were Edward Wallace of Shewalton, and his son Robert Wallace, Robert Mure of Knockmarloch, George Farquhar of Catrine and George Crawford, son of Robert Crawford of Smiddyshaw, all friends or kin or both. The witnesses at Irvine on 31st December were again Edward Wallace of Shewalton and his son Robert Wallace and Laurence Lynn of Bourtreehill.

It is interesting to note that this testament was given verbally by William to his father, Mungo, so did the witnesses hear directly from William or solely from Mungo? Also, was it first heard at Irvine at the end of December and at Shewalton the following May, or vice versa? No matter the order, this testament shows that William had been ill for many months.

It appears that William Reid's wife, Isobel Mure, was a Mure of Park since John Mure of Park is appointed tutor and overseer to William's children along with William's father, Mungo Reid. Park is in Tarbolton parish, and the Mures of Park are offshoots of the Mures of Rowallan. There is a fascinating reference to Park as the supposed 'Roman Trenches' marked on early Ordnance Survey maps are in fact a means of herding deer into a specific area, this is akin to discoveries at Falkland Palace.[68] Park would have been medieval hunting lands.

If John Mure of Park is Isobel's father, then her grandfather would be Bernard Mure who died at the battle of Fawsyde. '8th May 1548. John Mure, heir of Bernard Mure of Park, his father, who died under the flag of his majesty at the battle of Fawsyde in 40 soliditae of lands of Park, with the mill and its pertinents—viz., Sheipcoitleis, Parkhill, and Barhill, in the barony of Tarbolton.'[69]

On the 9th of September 1547 the inhabitants of Fawsyde Castle witnessed the battle of Little Fawsyde, a preliminary skirmish between the Scots and English cavalry, and after initial success the Scots were routed with a loss of 1300 men. The following day the Battle of Pinkie was fought. This conflict was between Somerset, Protector of England and the Earl of Arran, Regent of Scotland.[70] It sounds like a typical Scottish 'game,' snatching defeat from the jaws of victory. Mungo Mure of Rowallan also died at Pinkie so there was probably a large contingent of Mures fighting there. For many years this disastrous battle was commonly referred to as 'Black Satterday'.[71] Hew Campbell of Kingencleugh too died

68 Taylor, Simon 'Ayrshire Place-names: a rich seam still to mine' *Ayrshire Notes* 38, Autumn 2009 p13

69 Mure, William *The Works of Sir William Mure of Rowallan*, Vol.2 p303

70 www.battlefieldstrust.com

71 Mure, William *The Works of Sir William Mure of Rowallan*, Vol.2 p255

on 'Black Satterday'[72] and the Campbells of Kingencleugh, as we know, were close associates of Mungo Reid of Drumfork. Unfortunately, we do not know if Mungo or any of the Reids fought at this battle.

Testaments are not dry and dusty documents, much information can be gleaned from them and occasionally we get a chance to put some 'flesh onto the bones' and see family life in action. John Mure of Park died in October 1573 and his provision for his children shows a loving, caring father trying to do the best to provide for them all.[73] Edward Mure, his heir apparent, would obviously inherit the lands of Park. (Inheritance is not covered in testaments.) However, Edward was instructed to give the heritable right of all profits and duties of the lands which were held in wadset in the Lochliehill (*Lochlyhill*) to his brother, William Mure. Nor was William to receive his bairn's part as it was to be shared amongst his sisters so that they would receive a larger sum, the bairn's part was £167/19/2, a substantial sum in 1573. John Mure left all his moveable goods to his eldest daughter as well as instructions that the Northbog woods were to be sold and the income from this to go to her. Frustratingly the name of the elder daughter was left blank. Possibly this was the recently widowed Isabel Mure (married to William Reid) as her provision differed from her sisters who were 'lumped together' and treated the same while it appears that John Mure was making sure that his recently widowed daughter and her young family would have some sort of security. However, the four younger daughters were not forgotten, they were to receive part of Edward Mure's tocher when he married and if he died, they were to receive

72 Fergusson, Sir James *The Ayrshire Casualties at Pinkie*, p37

73 National Records of Scotland CC8/8/5

part of the tocher of their brother, William Mure.

The family relationships noted in John Mure of Park's testament goes some way to explaining Mungo Reid's kinship group. John Mure was married to Sibilla Wallace, daughter of Edward Wallace of Shewalton, and this Edward Wallace was appointed to be overseer and guide to Edward Mure and the rest of the Mure children, along with Robert Mure of Knockmarloch (possibly John Mure of Park's brother) and his mother, Agnes Stewart. And note the Shewalton connection and Mure witnesses of William Reid's testament. 'Kinship permeated all aspects of lifestyles and helped lesser lairds seeking employment or security. It was fundamental to testaments or wills and these kinship links through marriage could lead to interesting patterns of friendship or alliance.'[74] Kinship also included 'landholding, political alliances, moneylending, employment, cautioning, refuge from justice and care of children.'[75] All of which we see in the life of Mungo Reid and his family.

Another blow to Mungo in December 1572 was the death of his wife Mause Crawford. She is referred to as his 'sometime spous' indicating the length of their marriage rather than her being an occasional wife! Was the terminal illness of her eldest son William too much for an old lady to bear? Although dying in 1572 the Testament was only registered with the Edinburgh Commissary Court at the end of April 1583.[76] The Testament lists the goods and gear and sums of money of both Mause and Mungo at the time of her death, 80 bolls oats, 10 bolls beir (barley), 5 horses and mares, more

74 Meikle, Maureen M., *A British Frontier? Lairds and Gentlemen in the Eastern Borders, 1540-1603,* p25

75 Ibid. p32

76 National Records of Scotland CC8/8/12

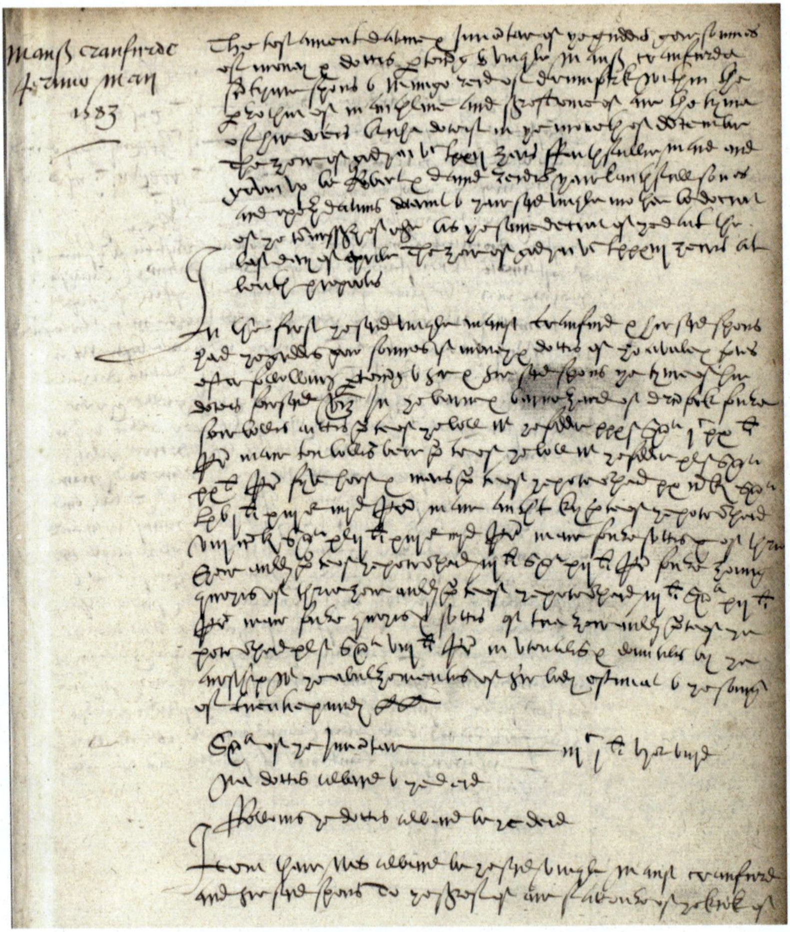

Fig. 10: Mause Crawford's Testament

than 8 cows, 4 more young bulls of 3 years old, 4 young heifers of 3 years old, 4 more heifers and young bulls of 2 years old and domestic goods and cloths. All this came to £30/6/8 and the executors were her sons Robert and David. Unfortunately, there is no surviving Testament for Mungo.

On 10th June 1582, we have a Precept of Clare Constat[77] in favour of Mungo Reid as heir to his deceased father, William Reid, son of Mungo Reid of Drumfork for the £3/6/8 lands of Drumfork, Brackenhill and Ballangape as well as the 2 merk lands of Glenbuck Eister. This grandson, Mungo (2), would have been about seven years old when his father William Reid died. This Precept also shows that Mungo (1) was still alive in June 1582.

We can assume that Mungo died sometime between June 1582 and April 1583 when Mause Crawford's testament was registered with the Edinburgh Commissary Court. The lands of Drumfork now passed to the next Mungo Reid (2).

Mungo and Mause appear to have had long and successful lives. They both reached old age, quite an achievement, surviving most of the sixteenth century. They had at least three sons and, no doubt, some daughters who would have been able to make profitable marriages which was the norm even at this level of society. Mungo had influential friends and family and appears to be of some social standing in Mauchline parish. He increased his land holding and progressed from tenant to feuar and successfully survived battles, skirmishes and feuds, not forgetting plague, disease, and periodic famines.

He was probably too young to have been at Flodden, but what of his father? He was at Linlithgow Bridge in January

77 Melrose Regality Records p307

1526, was he there at the September battle? Was he at Solway Muir or possibly Pinkie if his Mure kin were there? He lived through the minority of James V and his peer group were heavily involved with the Reformation in Ayrshire. He saw Mary Queen of Scots come and go. Did he fight for or against her or not at all?

Today as you stand on the lands of Drumfork and look down to the Dippol and across to the hills of New Cumnock and Black Crag, reputedly the haunt of Wallace, you are aware that the water courses have changed and the land has been enclosed but Mungo too would have looked to those hills.

Fig. 11: Hills from Drumfork

4

Mungo Reid 2 and 3

The new laird of Drumfork is the second Mungo Reid, grandson of Mungo and Mause and son of William Reid and Isabel Mure of Park. A laird could range from the great lairds with vast expanses of land and therefore wealth, power and status to the small bonnet laird. A laird was literally the 'lord' of his lands.[1] A laird normally held a minimum of two husbandlands of land, or fifty-two acres.[2] We know that Mungo owned about four hundred acres so perhaps being called a 'Gentleman of Kyle' is the most apt description.

Mungo was building on the solid foundations of his grandfather's good work. He was born about 1565 as a 1564 Charter shows that his parents were soon to be married.[3] The precept of Clare Constat dated 1582[4] shows him as heir to his grandfather's lands, and his father William's Testament of 1572[5] mentions his tutors, indicating that he was under 14 years. Boys under 14 and girls under 12 had tutors whereas boys over 14 and girls over 12 had curators to look after their interests. Even then it was known that girls mature earlier

1 Meikle, Maureen M., *A British Frontier? Lairds and Gentlemen in the Eastern Borders, 1540-1603*, p11

2 Ibid. p12

3 Yale University, Beinecke Rare Book and Manuscript Library Boswell Collection GEN MSS 89 Series XV oversize b.129 f.2380

4 Melrose Regality Records p307

5 National Record of Scotland CC9/7/30

than boys. Tutors were usually close family and as already mentioned, Mungo's were his grandfather Mungo (1) and John Mure of Park, probably his maternal grandfather. 'A tutor had to be over twenty-five, prudent in his own affairs and not be the immediate successor of his charge.'[6]

Mungo was married to Margaret Farquhar and sasine evidence shows this is the Farquhar of Gilmilnscroft family, a prestigious match, as the Farquhars were prominent local landowners. Even for this echelon of society marriages were arranged and formal legal contracts drawn up. It may have been a lucrative marriage but was it a happy one? Indeed, one example of how business-like marriage arrangements were is from an Instrument of 1529 when burgesses of Ayr, Alexander Farquhar, and his stepfather John Mure, arranged to pay forty pounds Scots each towards the tocher of Marion, John Mure's eldest daughter 'when she shall arrive at years of perfection' and if she died then his second daughter, Margaret, and so forth.[7]

Unfortunately, few records survive from this period, we really are doing detective work and gleaning as much information as we can from the documents. Some surviving sasines of Ovir Logan show Mungo's place in Kylesmure society and the complexities of landholding within and between local families and demonstrates that land meant income, no matter how small the piece of land. Ovir Logan, now in Sorn parish, is very close to Gilmilnscroft and was originally in the vast Mauchline parish, only a few miles from the lands of Drumfork.

6 Meikle, Maureen M., *A British Frontier? Lairds and Gentlemen in the Eastern Borders, 1540-1603,* p40

7 Anderson, Rev John, Grant, Francis J., *Protocol Book of Gavin Ros 1512-1532,* No. 879 p156

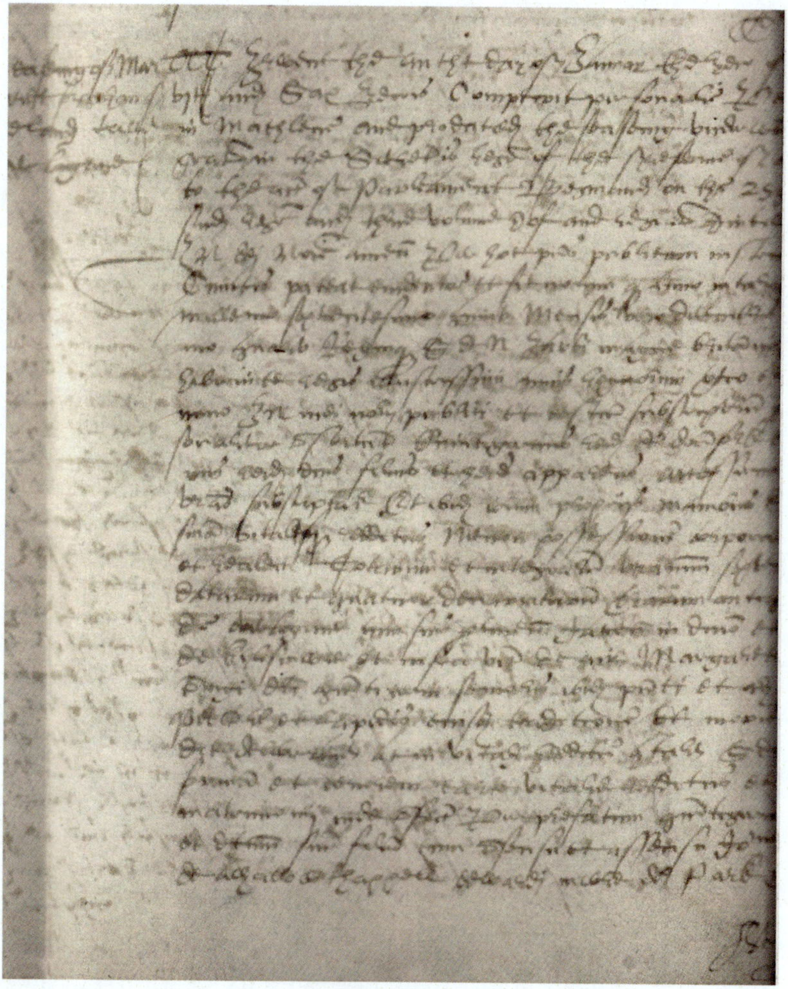

Fig. 12: Ovir Logan sasine, 1606.

A 1588[8] charter shows that Alexander Campbell of Barwhillan (*Barquhiling*) granted Mungo (2) the 17 shilling and 4 penny land of Ovir Logan. A 1606[9] sasine shows that this 17 shilling and 4 penny land of Ovir Logan was given in liferent to Margaret Farquhar as part of her marriage contract. This sasine also shows that Mungo (2) and Margaret have their son and heir, yet another Mungo. As this Mungo has curators his birth as well as his parents' marriage would need to be between 1585 and 1592. If Ovir Logan only came into Mungo's (2) hands in 1588, then it would appear likely that the marriage must be dated 1588 - 1592 and Mungo's (3) birth between these dates, possibly about 1590. Mungo (2) needed the consent of his son Mungo (3) and his son's curators to give the liferent of Ovir Logan to Margaret Farquhar 'for their interests'. Land and consequently income was tied up between family members and related families in quite complex patterns. It is interesting to note the names of Mungo's (3) curators, George Reid elder in Daldilling, John Reid elder of Ballochmyle, Edward Mure of Park and John Mure of Allhallowchapel, again demonstrating the close connection of the Reids of Drumfork, Daldilling and Ballochmyle and their family connections with the Mures of Park and Allhallowchapel in Tarbolton Parish.

Allhallowchapel is an interesting name and this John Mure, and his family witnessed several Drumfork documents. There was some difficulty in ascertaining its location, possibly it had some connection to the monastery at Fail, which is close to the lands of Park, however, there is also evidence of

8 Melrose Regality Records p338 No date given, however, looking at nearby entries it is probably 1588.

9 National Records of Scotland RS11/3/259

Mures at a Hollow Chappell near Dalrymple, and they are likely connected to the Mures of Auchendrane. Although to confuse matters further the Mures of Auchendrane were descendants of the Mures of Park.[10] A document of 1571/72, mentioning Torcross (*Torcors*) occupied by Mungo Mure of Allhallowchapel and his subtenants[11] and several other documents[12] confirmed that it was in Tarbolton parish. It would be interesting to know its exact location, possibly it could be the Chapel marked on Blaeu's map. Perhaps All Hallow ceased to be used once the Reformation took hold and Scotland lost so much of its Catholic heritage.

A sasine 'ceremony' took place on the actual land of Ovir Logan, sasine means 'seizing the earth' and earth and stones were handed over, no doubt refreshments too were consumed! The witnesses who attended the actual sasine ceremony were Robert Farquhar of Gilmilnscroft, James Mitchell younger of Turnerhill and George Farquhar of Catrine, landowners of a certain strata of Ayrshire society making sure their kinswoman received her legal due.

Ovir Logan is an area with which the Farquhar family had strong connections; a charter of 1580 shows them owning the 9 shilling and 2 penny portion.[13] There is also a sasine of 1602 showing that Mungo Reid sold the 8 shilling and 8 penny lands of Ovir Logan to John Mitchell of Dalgain.[14] Witnesses to this 1602 sasine ceremony are interesting, Robert Mitchell of Braehead, John Mitchell in Blackside (*Blacksyde*), William Smith in Bogend in Logan, Mungo Lennox in Logan, James

10 Paterson, James, *History of the County of Ayr,* vol.2 p361

11 National Records of Scotland RH6/2239

12 National Records of Scotland GD3/1/9/1

13 Melrose Regality Records p294

14 National Records of Scotland RS11/2/11

Henry (*Henrie*) in Syke (*Syik*) in Meiklewood and John Wilson in Whiteflat (*Qwhyitflut*). And note these names, Lennox, Henry and Wilson, as they will appear again later as tenants of Drumfork. As mentioned previously, to identify a piece of land a monetary sum of its value is given and the person who lives on it, often not the person who owned it. As this value had been calculated in the reign of Alexander III it did not reflect the current value. However, it is very interesting that so many small pieces of land can generate so many charters and sasines and this is just a fraction of the paperwork which has survived. Multiply this by all the landholding in Kylesmure, and on each pocket of land in these self-sufficient days, families would be 'drudging away' trying to earn a living.

We know that Mungo (2) sits on an Assise in Edinburgh on two occasions, possibly sitting on an Assise indicated that he was well thought of by his peer group. The first in 1596 is made up of Ayrshire men.[15] This was a land dispute between George Shaw (*Schaw*) of Glenmure and William Cunningham of Tourlands and the Assise found in favour of George Shaw. Interestingly, and just as a wee aside, William Cunningham of Tourlands was to lose his head a few years later, literally! He was part of a group that held the house of Cunninghamhead against the direct instructions of the king and was therefore found guilty of treason and beheaded at the market cross in Edinburgh.[16]

Mungo (2) was also on the Assise at the 1609 trial of notorious reivers Thomas Jardine (*Jardane*) of Birnok and his son Humphrey Jardine (*Umphra Jardane*).[17] They were being

15 *Register of the Great Seal of Scotland,* Vol.6 No. 463 p158

16 Edmonstone, Sir Archibald, *Genealogical Account of the Family of Edmonstone of Duntreath,* p44

17 Pitcairn, Robert, *Ancient Criminal Trials in Scotland,* Vol.3 p54

tried for a long list of crimes including the slaughter of William Campbell of Over Wellwood. Campbell was possibly known to Mungo as Wellwood at this time was still part of the large Mauchline parish, possibly this was why he was included on the Assise. This is a fascinating account of murder and gives an insight into life in early seventeenth century Ayrshire.

The Jardines were accused of a long list of crimes going back some twenty years. Most were for stealing horses, cattle, and sheep, e.g., the stealing of two horses, worth 100 merks each from Charles Murray as well as his 'cloik, sword, pistollis, steilbonnet and purse with sixty pounds therein'.[18]

However, one of their more notorious crimes was the burning of the place of Littlegill and the deaths of four of the occupants. There are several accounts of this, and others were involved, notably from the upper echelons of society who managed to wriggle out of facing justice. Blood feuds such as the Littlegill burning are multi-layered and go back many years.

There was also the slaughter of Robert Brown (*Broun*) at the Green of Coulter and stealing his horse worth £100 and the slaughter of John Tweedie (*Tuedie*) of Southwood upon Harelaw-mure beside St Ninian's Kirk. A local one is the stealing (articles not listed) from Hew Campbell, son of Hew Campbell in Garallan.

However, Thomas and Humphrey Jardine produced a Remission from the Crown dated 9th May 1605. Buying remissions from the crown was a common practice and guaranteed a pardon and freedom from prosecution. It was also, of course, a way for the crown to make money.

Thomas Jardine was also accused of the murder of

18 Ibid. p55

his own man, James Thomson 'binding him hand and fute' and throwing him into the Roberton burn to drown. Nasty! Another local one was Humphrey Jardine, for stealing a four-year-old brown horse worth 100 merks from Andrew Sloan (*Slowane*) in Lanehead from the lands of Waterhead in Cumnock. And, already mentioned, the slaughter of William Campbell of Wellwood 'committet be him and his complices at the Kirk of Douglas be hurting him, deidlie, in his heid and utheris pairtis of his body' in 1597 although he did not actually die until 1606.

The Jardines could not be tried for the crimes dated before 9th May 1605 due to their Crown Remission but they could face an Assise for the deaths of James Thomson and William Campbell. The Assise numbered some nineteen people and was one of the largest of any Criminal Trial in Scotland and, of course, it included Mungo Reid (2). By a majority of votes, Thomas Jardine was found guilty of the murder of his man James Thomson and Humphrey Jardine of William Campbell of Wellwood and they were acquitted of the other crimes. They were to be taken to the market cross of Edinburgh and their 'heidis were to be strukin frome thair bodeyis.'[19]

Scotland was beginning to calm somewhat under James VI and more so when he became James I of England and had more resources at his disposal to quell warring factions. Life, however, continued to be rather wild at times for those at Drumfork.

In October 1607 William Reid, a servant of Mungo Reid's son, gained a remission from James VI for his part in

19 Pitcairn, Robert, *Ancient Criminal Trials in Scotland,* Vol.3 p58

the murder of Laurence Rankine in Craig.[20] This murder had taken place in July of that year. Although a servant to Mungo's son, William Reid was possibly a member of the extended family. After much searching, no record of this incident can be found. Why was he murdered and how many took part in this? Would Mungo's son, or indeed Mungo (2) himself have been involved? And, who paid for the remission? Mungo's son, as you know another Mungo (3), was about seventeen when this incident happened.

However, of young Mungo (3) we know very little as tragically he died in 1617. History repeats itself and the lands of Drumfork would again pass to a grandson, and yes, yet another Mungo, the fourth that we know of. Mungo's (3) testament is dated 3rd May 1619[21] and the following month, June 1619, Mungo Reid (4) is mentioned in the Retour of Heirs as the legal heir to Drumfork.[22] Mungo's (3) testament shows that he had little in the way of belongings, 'no goods nor gear safe his clothes estimated at £10'. He died in late February 1617 having on the 21st told his father, Mungo Reid (2), his wishes and nominated him as tutor to his son Mungo (4). This implies that he knew he was dying but, from illness or injury we do not know. Certainly, it would appear to be something quite sudden as he had little time to put his affairs in order. An Andrew Mitchell in Mossgiel (*Mosgavill*) is cautioner for Mungo Reid (2) and his grandson. Possibly Andrew Mitchell in Mossgiel was the dead Mungo's (3) father-in-law, and we know that the Mitchells, like the Reids, the Farquhars and the Airds were prominent landowners in Mauchline parish.

20 *Register of the Great Seal of Scotland*, Vol.7 No.1122 p.413

21 National Records of Scotland CC9/7/15

22 Retours of Services of Heirs 1544-1699 Inquisitionem ad capellam domini regis retornatarum abbreviatio Inquisitiones Generales 843

As well as feuding and murder we also find evidence of adultery. In February 1615 Mungo Reid (2) who is married to Margaret Farquhar gained a remission from the king for adultery with Janet (*Jonete*) Reid, the sister of Hugh Reid in Thirdpart.[23] One can assume that the evidence of adultery is the birth of a child. Although the remission was dated 1615 no indication is given of when the adultery took place. Thirdpart is only a couple of miles from Drumfork so fine and handy to saddle up your horse and ride across. Possibly Janet Reid was not his only extra-marital relationship. Confusingly, there was also a Thirdpart near Barskimming in Mauchline parish, so maybe his horse had to journey a few more miles. And 'our' Mungo was not alone as in January of the same year a John Reid in Merkland and a William Reid in Mossgiel were granted remission for adultery with their servants, Janet Richard (*Janeta Richert*) and Elizabeth Anderson respectively. Serving girls have always been easy prey.[24]

The amount of extra marital activity appears to be commonplace as well as the number of illegitimate births, especially to 'men of the Church'. Records of the Privy Seal shed light on several illegitimacies and subsequent legitimisations. Of interest are those of Sir William Reid, chaplain in Mauchline. In 1583/84 there was a precept of legitimation of Mungo Reid, burgess of Canongate and his brother, Alexander, sons of the deceased Sir William Reid, chaplain in Mauchline.[25] Possibly Sir William Reid, chaplain at Mauchline, was related to the Reids of Drumfork as we do have an Alexander Reid burgess of the Canongate appearing in later legal documents, and

23 *Register of the Great Seal of Scotland,* Vol.7 No.1178 p.435
24 Ibid. Vol.7 No.1173 p.432
25 *Register Privy Seal,* Vol. VIII No.1896

Mungo is a family Christian name. There were also several legitimisations for Sir John Reid the curator at Auchinleck Church. On March 10th, 1583/84, 'a precept of legitimation of Adam Reid in Heilar, son of the deceased Sir John Reid, curator of the parish church of Auchinleck and of Christina Reid, daughter of the said Sir John.'[26]

There is evidence of locals being involved in the Plantation of Ulster. In 1626, John Reid, a great grandson of our first Mungo sold Hern (one of the small pockets of land making up the modern Drumfork) to Thomas Ferguson, the blacksmith there, as he had settled in the Kingdom of Ireland.[27] At this time James Reid of Willoxhill had also moved to Ireland. Although we only have a small mention in a sasine, John Reid and James Reid would no doubt have taken their wives and retainers with them. Tom Devine states, 'The Scots who made the move to Ulster seem to have been a relatively balanced cross-section of the national population. At the upper end of the scale were small landowners and substantial tenants who saw the venture as an unprecedented opportunity for economic advancement... below this élite class was a broad social spread which included artisans and labourers as well as farm servants and cottars. Significantly for every four men, three women moved to Ulster... this was an important influence which helped to maintain the distinctive identity of the Ulster Scots.'[28] It is well documented that Montgomery of Eglinton held vast lands in Ulster to which many of his Ayrshire tenants moved. However, in 1609 Henry Stewart of Barskimming (married to Janet Reid second

26 *Register Privy Seal,* Vol. VIII No. 1910

27 National Records of Scotland GD1/186/8

28 Devine, T. M., *Scotland's Empire 1600–1815,* p24

Fig. 13: Brackenhill

daughter of Adam Reid of Barskimming) had a grant of 2000 acres in Ulster.[29] (This is what makes doing this research so interesting. We get a wee snippet of information and then want to find out more. The Plantations of Ulster is still to be pursued in greater depth.)

The charter for the sale of Hern[30] had been written by Mr Andrew Dalrymple at Ayr on 26th June 1626 and we shall hear more of the Dalrymples in due course. A human touch is that John Reid could not write his name and his hand was 'led by the pen of the notary,' William Mitchell. The witnesses to the charter were John Mure of Hallowchapel, Robert Reid,

29 *Cracroft's Peerage*, online, Lords Avondale and Ochiltree entry
30 National Records of Scotland RS12/4/378

messenger in Ayr, James Reid in Pennyland and Adam Aird in Mauchline, familiar names. However, it was in March 1629 at Irvine that James Fergusson of Auchenbrain (*Auchinbrayne*) presented the Instrument of Sasine. Thomas Fergusson the blacksmith in Hern was present as was Mungo Reid, acting as baillie. At the actual sasine ceremony on the lands of Hern, Mungo Reid gave Thomas Fergusson a handful of earth and stones, and the witnesses were John Dalziel (*Daillzeill*) in Mauchline, Charles Murdoch (*Murdoche*) in Drumfork, Alexander Thomson in Hill and Thomas Richard (*Richeart*) in Knokdows.

A 1625 Sasine[31] shows that Brackenhill was granted by Mungo (2) to George Reid and Elizabeth Mure as part of their marriage contract. An auspicious date, 1625, the year Charles I becomes king, therefore, we know where all this is heading. George Reid is one of Mungo's (2) sons and Elizabeth Mure is of the family of Mure of Middleton (*Middiltoun*) as a William Mure of Middleton acted as baillie for this transaction, possibly her father or brother. Middleton is in Tarbolton parish and close to the lands of Park. In this Sasine, Mungo Reid (2) represented his young grandson Mungo (4) who would be about ten years old. Witnesses to the sasine ceremony itself were Adam Aird in Catrine, John Aird in Nether Heateth, John Pedin (*Pathene*) in Nether Heateth and Robert Wilson in Drumfork, all very local and not having far to travel.

By the seventeenth century we are noting the tenants, names such as Wilson and Pedin, still in existence in the Census returns of the nineteenth century. Class distinctions were never strong in Scotland and landed families were bound

31 National Records of Scotland RS12/3/403

to each other by kinship and the land itself. 'Between the laird and his tenant and even his servant there remained a kinship of feeling, a realisation of common interest, a sense of loyalty to the soil on which and from which both of them lived.'[32] 'The sharp division between lord and tenant in England was an anathema of Scottish lairds who had strong feelings of paternalism and mutual respect for blood-related kinsmen, their surname group and allies (who were not necessarily related to the laird or even called by his surname.)'[33]

Mungo (2) died about 1634, in his seventies, a good age for this period. In his long life he seemed to have continued the good work of his grandfather in maintaining his lands and his status within his peer group. There was greater stability in the country even though the centre of power had shifted from Edinburgh to London. What were his thoughts on the execution of a queen? Would he have approved of James VI hightailing off to England and Scotland now being part of Great Britain? And what would he have thought of Charles I and the growing unrest in the country?

32 Fergusson, Sir James of Kilkerran, *Lowland Lairds,* p15

33 Meikle, Maureen M., *A British Frontier? Lairds and Gentlemen in the Eastern Borders 1540-1603,* p24

5

Mungo Reid 4

Control of Drumfork now passed to the fourth Mungo Reid. And what a time to be alive, with the signing of the National Covenant and the Wars of the Three Kingdoms looming. Mungo was born about 1615, his father Mungo (3), having died in 1617 and his mother was possibly the daughter of Andrew Mitchell in Mossgiel. The Mitchell family like the Reids were widespread throughout Kylesmure.

It appeared that Mungo made quite a prestigious marriage to Isobell Boswell second daughter of David Boswell the fifth Laird of Auchinleck.[1] David Boswell had married Isobell Wallace in 1613 and an indication of their social standing was their eldest daughter Marion marrying Alan, Lord Cathcart, Jane, their third daughter marrying John Gordon, younger of Earlston and Margaret their fourth daughter David Blair of Adamstown.[2] However, there was a discrepancy as to which Isobell Boswell Mungo actually married, far from unusual with a dearth of surviving records. It has now been confirmed that he married Isobel Boswell the eighth child of James Boswell, the fourth laird and his wife Marion Crawford, who had married around 1590.[3] In a sasine of 1636 Isobell Boswell is referred to as the sister of David

1 Ducharme, Diane J., *Guide to the Boswell Collection GEN MSS 89*, Yale University Library Beinecke Rare Book and Manuscript Library p8

2 Ibid. p9

3 Boswell J. J., *History and Genealogical Table of the Boswells*

Fig. 14: Old Place of Auchinleck

Fig. 15: Old Place of Auchinleck

Boswell of Auchinleck.[4] Marriage to the eighth child of the fourth laird of Auchinleck is more appropriate as Mungo Reid (4) was a small laird and not of the rank of the spouses of the fifth laird's daughters. The 1651 marriage contract of Isobell Boswell and John Shaw of Sornbeg confirmed that she was indeed the daughter of the fifth laird, and there had been no previous marriage to Mungo Reid.[5] (This marriage contract was in an Italian Archive, the Fondazione Sella, and they have been very helpful in sending me a copy. Jasper John Boswell's daughter married into the Sella family and his paperwork is now archived there.)

---

4 National Records of Scotland RS12/6/538-539r

5 Isobell Boswell and John Shaw of Sornbeg Marriage Contract 1651. Courtesy of the Fondazione Sella, Biella

What sort of dwelling would have been at Drumfork? Isobell Boswell would not have moved from the 'Old Place' of Auchinleck to a 'hovel'. The Reids of Drumfork must have lived in a building of some substance. Blaeu's map does not show a tower at Drumfork although it does for the Reids' peer group at Daldilling, Smiddyshaw, Ballochmyle, Barskimming, Park and Mossgiel. If there was not a tower, then possibly there would have been a bastle house.[6] Unfortunately, there is no evidence of any previous structure at the modern Drumfork, either it was built over or was on the slightly higher ground to the east of the farmstead. However, the 1564 Charter of Mungo Reid for William Reid[7] mentions the 'mansion house of Drumfork' and although 'mansion house' is standard terminology it does indicate that the Reids of Drumfork had a dwelling of some significance.

Mungo Reid (4) took control of his lands in 1636 and one can see immediately that things are not going well financially. A sasine for Drumfork, Brackenhill, Ballangape and Ovir Logan,[8] dated 18th October 1636, shows that Mungo's (4) grandfather had died in 1634. It states that there had been an inquest held in Chancery at the command of Charles I as the land had been in the king's hand for two years. Mungo was described as a 'discreet man of full age and legal heir to his grandfather'. There was outstanding feu duty of some £40/17/5. A John Mowat was baillie and the sasine was written by William Mitchell, notary and clerk of the diocese of Glasgow. Witnesses of the sasine ceremony itself were Matthew Boswell in Mauchline, George Reid in

6 Sanderson, M. H. B., pers. comm.

7 Yale University, Beinecke Rare Book and Manuscript Library Boswell Collection GEN MSS 89 Series XV oversize b.129 f.2380

8 National Records of Scotland RS12/6/535

Auchenlongford (*Auchlanford*), Mathew Reid the notary in Mauchline and John Aird in Auchenlongford. If his land had been in resignation to the king for two years, Mungo would have earned nothing from it as all rentals etc. would have gone to the Crown.

A Boswell is now appearing as part of the extended family. Isobell Boswell had an illegitimate half-brother, Matthew. When her father died in 1618 his testament stated that Matthew, his natural son, was to have 'three of the best ky in the byre'. Her mother was left 'the stand bed in the young laird's chalmer that he lies in and the ane laich bed nearest the window in the old laird's chalmer.' Shades of Shakespeare who left his second best bed to his wife, Anne Hathaway![9]

Two days later, 20th October 1636, there is another instrument of sasine granting Isobell Boswell the liferent of the thirty shilling and four pence lands of Drumfork and Ballangape.[10] Presumably Mungo reached full age in 1636 when his lands were returned from the king, and the liferent for his wife would have been part of their marriage contract. Again, John Mowat in Newton (*Newtoun*) of Ayr was baillie and Matthew Reid, notary in Mauchline, had drawn up the document. Witnesses to the sasine ceremony, where Isobell Boswell was ceremoniously handed some earth and stones, were Matthew Boswell in Mauchline, William Mitchell, notary, George Reid in Brackenhill and William Lennox in Drumfork. Here we have the first mention of a William Lennox who is married to an Agnes Henry and is probably related to the Mungo Lennox who had lived in Ovir Logan in the early 1600s.

---

9 Paterson, James *History of the County of Ayr,* Vol.1 p239

10 National Records of Scotland RS12/6/538-539r

Within a few months there is more legal paperwork. On the 16th of March 1637 Margaret Farquhar, widow of Mungo Reid (2), presented a Bond of Obligation giving her an annual life rent of twenty-two merks and nine shillings Scots to be uplifted from the lands of Drumfork and Ballangape. To oversee all this Robert Farquhar elder of Gilmilnscroft, no doubt a close relative of Margaret, had been appointed baillie by Mungo Reid on 5th January 1637.[11] The witnesses show the extended family ties as well as the tenant families. For the sasine document George Reid of Brackenhill, John Reid in Raith (*Raithe*), Alexander Reid, burgess of Edinburgh and Matthew Reid, notary and the sasine ceremony George Reid of Brackenhill, William Lennox in Drumfork, William Wilson in Logan and Laurence Vallance (*Vallans*) servitor to Mungo Reid.

Unfortunately, Mungo is struggling to hold it all together and debts are piling up. The liferent of Brackenhill goes to his uncle George and the liferent of Drumfork and Ballangape to his wife Isobell Boswell and his widowed grandmother Margaret Farquhar. Probably he was also suffering from the knock-on effects of savage taxation and a depreciation of currency, as well as a series of bad harvests. Mungo is not alone in struggling, 'at his coming to the estate he found it very low and almost sunk burdened with liferents, dowries and numerous other debts.'[12] This describes David Boswell, sixth laird of Auchinleck but could just as easily apply to 'our' Mungo. When David Boswell (fifth laird) died in 1661, his daughters did not inherit, and the estate passed

11 National Records of Scotland RS12/7/28

12 Ducharme, Diane J., *Guide to the Boswell Collection* GEN MSS 89, Yale University Library Beinecke Rare Book and Manuscript Library p10

to his nephew David Boswell.[13] The remaining daughters did bring legal proceedings to be recognised as heirs and lost.

The situation at Drumfork continues to deteriorate. At Christmas 1639 Mungo wadsets part of the Mains of Drumfork to William Campbell, portioner of Hillhouse and heirs failing to his brother George Campbell of Shaw (*Schaw*).[14] Wadsetting was a way of formally and legally transferring possession of land for a monetary sum, and, of course, we are working in a society without banks. (Interestingly in old Scots a female moneylender was a wad-wyfe.[15]) The land involved was a merkland of the Mains of Drumfork occupied by Agnes Henry and William Lennox. Witnesses to this charter of 25th December 1639 were Matthew Reid and William Mitchell, notaries in Mauchline, John Reid officer in Catrine and William Ferguson the blacksmith in Hern. The sasine which followed on 1st January 1640 mentions Andrew Mitchell in Meiklewood as baillie and witnesses James Marshall in Mauchline, John Reid, son of John Reid officer in Catrine and others unnamed.

Only a few days later, 11th January 1640, the 17 shilling and 4 penny lands of Ovir Logan was sold to Robert Farquhar younger of Gilmilnscroft.[16] The baillie for this was John Gemmill in Gilmilnscroft. The precept of sasine, written by Matthew Reid notary in Mauchline, was witnessed at Mauchline by James Marshall, merchant in Mauchline, as well

13 Ibid. p10

14 National Records of Scotland RS12/7/275 & Ayr Particular Register of Sasines & The Clan Campbell, Abstract of Entries relating to Campbells in the Early Unprinted records Relating to Ayrshire 1515-1650. Vol.V p108

15 Greig, Andrew, *Rose Nicolson*, p449

16 National Record of Scotland RS/7/318r-318v

Fig. 16: Rainbow over Drumfork

as John Mason (*Massoun*) and William Campbell. The sasine ceremony at Ovir Logan was performed by John Gemmill giving earth and stones to Robert Farquhar. Witnesses were Robert Farquhar eldest son to Robert Farquhar younger, his brother Alexander Farquhar, John Bar and John Curle.

There is no pot of gold at the end of the rainbow for Mungo, he struggles on for another six years, but the downward spiral continues. In April 1646 another two merklands of the Mains of Drumfork occupied by William Lennox is wadset to George Campbell of Shaw.[17] This charter was witnessed by Robert Farquhar of Gilmilnscroft, George Farquhar portioner of Catrine and Andrew Dalrymple and Matthew Reid notaries in Mauchline. Of interest, the wife of

17 National Record of Scotland RS12/8/37

George Campbell of Shaw is Christian Farquhar, no doubt a Farquhar of Gilmilnscroft. The baillie for the sasine ceremony was John Campbell younger of Kingencleugh giving sasine to George Campbell and his son William. Witnesses were Robert Farquhar of Gilmilnscroft, William Lennox in Drumfork and John Duncan and James Beg in Clewes.

The wolves are getting ready to pounce. However, we are in the throes of the Wars of the Three Kingdoms. In 1643 Robert Farquhar of Gilmilnscroft had been appointed by Parliament as a Commissioner of Ayrshire and one of his first tasks was to assess landowners for payment towards a loan of 1,200,000 merks and another of 100,000 merks for defraying the expenses that had occurred in the sending of an army of 10,000 soldiers to Ireland to supress the rebellion there.[18] Mungo Reid, no doubt, had to contribute to the rebellion/wars from dwindling returns as he sells off his assets.

Debt in pre banking society is a fascinating subject. Personal debt between people is huge and can continue for many years and pass down the generations. Land was collateral and everyone seemed to owe someone money. Testaments are 'gold dust' for detecting who owed what to whom at this level of society, from a little amount to spectacular sums e.g., from the Testament of Margaret Campbell in Holehouse (*Hoilhous*) in February 1612[19] we see that her estate is valued at £288/13/4, and she is owed £341/6/8 by several people including Adam Reid in Heilar, David Durie of Heilar and Mungo Reid of Drumfork. Contrast this with the 1623 Testament of Hew

18 Robertson, George, *A genealogical account of the principal Families in Ayrshire*, Vol. II p53

19 Paton (editor) *The Clan Campbell, Abstract of Entries relating to Campbells in the Early Unprinted records Relating to Ayrshire 1515-1650.* Vol.V p165

Campbell, Lord of Loudoun[20] whose estate is valued at £9640 but was owed £21558 by many people including Agnes Reid, widow of John Campbell of Kingencleugh, George Reid of Daldilling, John Reid of Ballochmyle, Hugh Reid in Thirdpart and, of course, 'our' Mungo Reid of Drumfork. Mungo was also mentioned the year previously in the 1622 Testament of John Campbell, baillie of Mauchline,[21] whose estate was valued at a mere £10 but was owed some £967/17/8 by a considerable number including Mungo Reid of Drumfork.

Of course, the Mungo Reid of Drumfork referred to above is Mungo (2) but Mungo (4) seemed to have followed the same pattern as his grandfather. The 1643 Testament of Hew Campbell of Netherplace[22] whose estate was valued at £861/6/8 was owed some £4537/17/10 by a substantial number including Mungo Reid of Drumfork, and this is just a sample of the numerous testaments that exist. A more poignant one perhaps, reminding us that we are dealing with flesh and blood people, is the 1627 Testament of an Elizabeth Campbell daughter of the deceased Charles Campbell of Horsecleugh (*Horscleuche*) in Cumnock parish[23] whose estate is valued at £10 'she being a young woman unmarried, having only two sheep and a lamb and her clothing'.

Mungo's situation remained perilous and by 1649 Brackenhill was sold to Adam Aird of Catrine.[24] Dated 6th February 1649 and registered at Irvine on 15th February, Adam Aird, portioner of Catrine with his wife Anna Boswell and their son William, presented a charter containing a

20 Ibid. p188
21 Ibid. p185
22 Ibid. p208
23 Ibid. p196
24 National Records of Scotland RS12/8/209v

precept of sasine of the 23 shillings and 4 penny lands of Brackenhill which was occupied by George Reid and had been granted to them by Mungo Reid. The baillie was John Reid of Ballochmyle, William Crawford of Poshill a witness, and Matthew Reid again the notary. At the sasine ceremony were Adam Aird, his wife and son and witnesses John Aird in Heateth, George Allan (*Allane*) in Yett, his brother Hugh Allan and John Miller in Landsyde. Possibly Anna Boswell was connected to Isobell. A Disposition of the sasine overleaf, dated December 1648[25] gives a detailed insight to the debts and affairs of Mungo Reid.

By 1650 Mungo (4) had gone under completely and disponed (transferred) Drumfork and Ballangape to a Charles Dalrymple.[26] Charles Dalrymple set about paying off what was owed to the Campbells of Shaw, as on 1st March 1650 there was a registration of renunciation by George Campbell of Shaw and his son William Campbell for the wadset parts of the Mains of Drumfork, Charles Dalrymple having paid 4200 merks to redeem the land.[27]

Aged about thirty-five Mungo Reid had lost it all. Presumably he continued at Drumfork as a tenant. Although having descended the social scale, the lot of small lairds and bigger tenants was not too dissimilar.

What a tumultuous time he had lived through. Standing up to the king had led to revolution and a Covenanter government. Almost the whole country was swept along on a tide of euphoria with the signing of the National Covenant in 1638. The Covenanter government reached

25 Yale Beinecke Rare Book and Manuscript Library GEN MSS 89 Series XVI Box 137 Folder 2502 Disposition to Adam Aird 1648

26 National Records of Scotland RS12/8/291

27 Paton, Henry (Editor), *The Clan Campbell Abstracts,* Vol.V p132

Fig. 17: Disposition of Brackenhill, 1648 (top half above and bottom half on facing page)

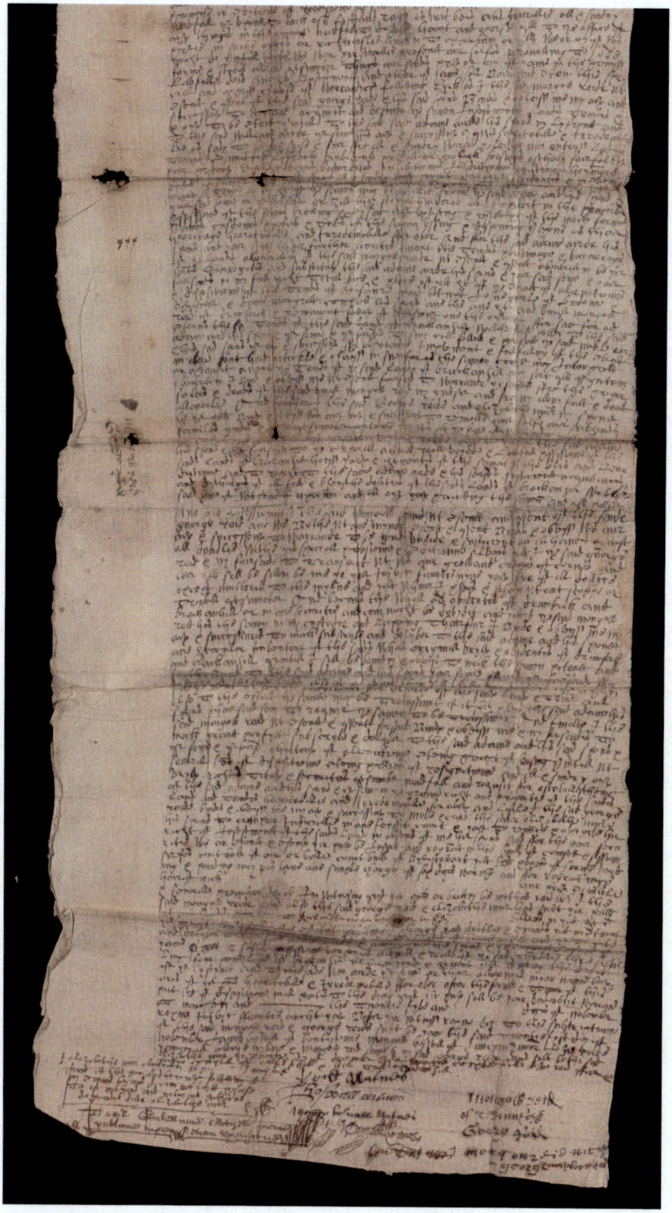

the apex of their power in 1643, liaising with the English parliament and imposing the Solemn League and Covenant, which they believed had established Presbyterianism across Britain. Scotland had supplied troops to Ireland to quell the rebellion and to England to fight onside with the English parliamentarians, that Scottish Covenanter troops were integral to victory at Marston Moor in 1644 is largely forgotten. Scottish troops had fought in Europe during the Thirty Years War with Gustavus Adolphus, and honed their martial skills. On their return to Scotland they formed the basis of well trained and disciplined force with experienced commanders. Indeed, three of Isobell Boswell's brothers fought with Adolphus in Sweden and never returned to Scotland.[28]

However, by 1650, the country was war weary and there had been a huge loss of men, either dying in battle or taken prisoner and transported to the English colonies, few would return to Scotland. 'Between 1642 and 1651 about one fifth to one quarter of the adult male population of Scotland was lost, men in the prime of their life.'[29] Isobell had lost her brother, Captain John Boswell, 'slain in the wars in England.'[30]

Mungo and Isobell had lived through all this and survived, although far from unscathed. Doubtless they signed the National Covenant. However, with skirmishes and battles, growing debt and finally insolvency, the repercussions of the Wars of the Three Kingdoms had a profound effect on their lives.

The Reids, tenants then feuars, 'Gentlemen of Kyle' for

28 Paterson, James, *History of the County of Ayr*, Vol.1 p238

29 Haggart, Craig, *The demographic impact of the Civil Wars on Scotland*

30 Paterson, James, *History of the County of Ayr*, Vol.1 p238

almost a century, finally lost Drumfork. Four hundred years on that sense of loss can still be felt.

6

Dalrymples and Airds at Drumfork

Charles Dalrymple now owns Drumfork. He is of a wealthy family of lawyers, the eldest son of Andrew Dalrymple, a notary in Mauchline and servitor to Lord Loudoun. On first discovering that Andrew Dalrymple was Loudoun's 'servant' the assumption was made that he was a member of the house staff, not his legal representative and 'right-hand' man appearing to be crucial to the functioning of Loudoun's household. Previously Dalrymple had worked for the Duchess of Lennox, Lord Loudoun's sister.

The following extract gives an interesting snapshot of life in this echelon of society and the role of Andrew Dalrymple.[1] In February 1616 there was a proclamation of James VI's intention to visit Scotland the following year, therefore, there was to be 'no hunting or shooting of deer, hare, and wild fowl within eight miles of Glasgow until September 1617' so that there might be plenty of game for the 'recreation of his majesty and his retinue'. In anticipation of this visit several lords appeared before the Privy Council to report on who may have misplaced a royal tapestry. Lord Loudoun stated that Andrew Dalrymple, who had been a servant to his sister, the late Duchess of Lennox, could explain what had become of any royal tapestry or any other effects that may have been in her possession. Dalrymple, under oath, said that there

1 Marwick, J.D. (Editor), *British History Online Charters and documents relating to the city of Glasgow 1175-1649 Part 1.*

was a chamber 'within the dungeon of the castle of Glasgow' (meaning a room and not a subterranean cell) hung with tapestry as well as a silk bed and that on her removal from the castle, the duchess 'kept all her moveables and household stuff within it' and that the archbishop of St Andrew's, formerly archbishop of Glasgow, and James Stewart in Glasgow 'mellit' with the said castle and all that was within it by direction from the Duke of Lennox. It was not a happy marriage! Lennox is reportedly to have said, 'ther is no powar in earthe that can make me to use her as a wife.' Lennox abandoned her and the children of her first marriage and escaped to London with his own daughter taking everything of value leaving his wife 'in a very sober state'. Sadly, when she died in 1609 her brother had to grudgingly arrange and pay for her funeral.[2]

Was Andrew Dalrymple a Loudoun man looking after Loudoun's interests, even those of his estranged sister? Indeed, in November 1626 Andrew Dalrymple was curator along with John, Lord of Loudoun to Elizabeth Campbell, daughter of the deceased George Campbell, master of Loudoun.[3] Working for an aristocratic family, and possibly having a pension guaranteeing an annual income, gave ready access to money which could be lent out, obviously with interest. Lawyers would be aware of those who were struggling financially and could move in to help, acquiring property if bills could not be settled.[4] We see this clearly with Charles Dalrymple and the lands of Drumfork and Andrew Dalrymple with the lands of Stair, belonging to James Dalrymple.

The *Oxford Dictionary of National Biography*[5]

2 Brown, Keith M., *Noble Society in Scotland,* p153

3 National Records of Scotland GD112/3/60

4 Baptie, Diane, *A Lairdship Lost; The Mowats of Balquholly,* p23

5 *Oxford Dictionary of National Biography* Online re James Dalrymple

mentions Andrew Dalrymple in the entry for James Dalrymple, first Viscount Stair (1619-1695). 'Viscount Stair's formal connection with the legal profession began on 17th February 1648, when Dalrymple was admitted as an advocate in the college of justice, though he may have been related to Andrew Dalrymple, a notary public in Mauchline, who appears in several records as 'servitor' to the Earl of Loudoun and who was sufficiently prosperous to act as guarantor for the payment of Loudoun's debts. In 1624 Dalrymple's patrimonial estate had been mortgaged to Andrew Dalrymple, and one of the first things he did on being admitted to the bar was to redeem the mortgage on 1st March 1648. A Glasgow graduate himself, Andrew Dalrymple sent one of his sons to the university in 1643, and it is possible that his success as a lawyer had some influence on James Dalrymple's decision to enter the legal profession.'

Andrew Dalrymple and his sons are connected to the Dalrymples of Stair, the exact relationship uncertain, but the Dalrymples of Stair were indeed a family on the ascendant. Andrew Dalrymple graduated from Glasgow University in 1597.[6] In 1611 he married Janet Dalrymple the only child of Charles Dalrymple one of the quartermasters of Ayr and his second wife Janet Brown.[7] This Charles Dalrymple had died of plague in 1606,[8] and although there were periodic outbreaks, 1606-9 proved to be a rather severe epidemic in Ayrshire. Shearer states that Andrew Dalrymple belonged to a family of some prominence since his cautioners were James

first Viscount Stair

6 Glasgow University Archives

7 Shearer, J. D., *Ayr and its People,* p125

8 Ibid. p50

Boswell of Auchinleck and David Dunbar of Enterkine.[9]

From a sasine of 1639[10] we learn that Andrew Dalrymple and his wife Janet, lived in Mauchline on the twenty-penny land of Green (*Grein*) and its park, this included a tenement of land with a garden lying on its east side, all lying within the ten-pound lands of Mauchline Mains, Green is still evident in modern Mauchline place names. On their deaths this land was to pass to their second son John and his heirs whom failing his brother Andrew and his heirs. This rather complex document mentions several names: the Earl of Loudoun as superior of the lands, David Dunbar of Enterkine as a witness, Charles Dalrymple and his servitors, John Haldane (*Halden*) and Alexander Kerr (*Kar*). The other occupants of Green alongside Andrew and Janet Dalrymple were Robert Reid, William Millikine, William Wilson, and the deceased James Crawford (a bit of a stench surely?). Robert Wallace, burgess of Ayr, was baillie, and at the sasine ceremony were Andrew and Janet Dalrymple with witnesses Alexander Campbell and Thomas Fisher, both merchants in Mauchline, William Millikine, and James Davie a servitor to Andrew Dalrymple. However, within five years John Dalrymple with the approval of his father had granted his brother Charles, and his new wife Jean Hume (*Hoome*) as part of their marriage contract, ' six acres of land on the outskirts of Mauchline and a small enclosed meadow, a grain yard and a yard which for some time had belonged to George Campbell in Burnside, as well as the aforementioned 'twenty penny lands of old extent of Green and its green with houses and buildings thereon lying in Mauchline and a tenement of land and yard lying on the

9 Ibid. p126

10 National Records of Scotland RS12/7/278

east side of the stream with the houses thereon occupied by Mr Andrew Dalrymple, William Millikine, Robert Reid, John Crawford (son of the deceased James?) and William Wilson, all lying within the ten pound lands of Mauchline Mains'.[11]

Another indication of the wealth of the Dalrymple family is evidenced from a sasine dated 24th June 1645, the same day as the above. In this Andrew Dalrymple grants Charles Dalrymple 'the four merkland of old extent of Bibblonwood (*Bublionwood*) called Halls (*Haillis*), (possibly near Muirkirk as there is a Bibblon Hill) fifty-five soums of grass in the North Mure which had sometime been occupied by John Gibson and now John Anderson.' As well as the movement of land amongst his sons, we learn from Shearer that Andrew and Janet Dalrymple had several houses in Ayr inherited from her father and great uncle, one on the Sea Vennel next door to what is now Loudoun Hall.[12]

It seems that all of Andrew Dalrymple's sons went to university. A procuratory of resignation of the Lands of Shiell, barony of Kyle, dated 8th January 1668,[13] shows that 'our Charles Dalrymple of Drumfork' was a lawyer and clerk to the Sasines of Ayr, although we do not know the date of his graduation. He was married to Jean Hume and records show that from 1650 he is designated of Drumfork and from about 1659 of Waterside. (His son was Charles Dalrymple of Langlands, writer in Kilmarnock, factor to the Earl of Kilmarnock in 1688 and a baillie of the Barony of Kilmarnock and Town Councillor in 1695.[14]) John, Andrew Dalrymple's second son was a lawyer and a notary in Irvine. James who

11 National Records of Scotland RS12/8/21

12 Shearer, J. D., *Ayr and its People*, p125

13 National Records of Scotland GD 135/466

14 Shaw, John, *The Dalrymples of Langlands*, p1

graduated in 1643 was also a lawyer and Andrew, graduating from Glasgow University in 1646, was minister at Auchinleck and then Sorn (Dalgain).

We know that by 1650 Mungo Reid had disponed Drumfork to Charles Dalrymple. From a document of 1658[15] we learn that Charles then passed Drumfork to his brother, Andrew Dalrymple, minister at Auchinleck. It is dated the 28th December 1658 and starts with John Dalrymple, writer in Irvine and brother of Charles, producing a document that had been written on the 7th December showing a letter of alienation containing a sasine by which Charles Dalrymple granted his brother, Andrew Dalrymple minister at Auchinleck, 2000 merks annual rent to be uplifted by him from the ten merkland of the lands of Terringzean as the principal lands and the lands of Drumfork, Hern and Ballangape as the warrandice lands. This letter of alienation uses the lovely term 'my lovitts', usually used by king to subjects, but again, this was brothers. Another of the Dalrymple brothers, James Dalrymple of Pennyfadzeoch mill (*milne*), was baillie for this transaction. This is a complex and fascinating document illustrating again the movement of land between the siblings yet retaining wealth within the family. (And, yes, I have had to research Scottish Law of this period to try and make sense of what is going on!) The sasine ceremony at Terringzean at 2.00pm was witnessed by Andrew and John Gemmill in Lanaid, Ninian Dalrymple in Waterside and John Mure in Terringzean. And at Drumfork, Hern and Ballangape at 3.00pm or thereabouts, obviously when they had finished their dram and saddled up their horses to ride the couple of miles to Drumfork, witnessed again by Ninian Dalrymple, George Simpson weaver in

15 National Records of Scotland RS13/3/402

Fig. 18: Auchinleck Kirk

Dippolburn (*Drippilburne*), Quintein Dick servant to George Dalrymple in Hill and William McAdam, son to William McAdam notary in Ayr. It is likely that Ninian Dalrymple in Waterside and George Dalrymple in Hill are members of the extended Dalrymple family.

Waterside owned by Charles Dalrymple and Pennyfadzeoch mill owned by his brother James now form part of the Dumfries House estate. It appears, therefore, that there were Dalrymples living there a century before William Crichton-Dalrymple commenced the building of his grand new Dumfries House. The Dalrymples were indeed a family of 'movers and shakers' in the upper echelons of Ayrshire society.

Fig. 19: Sorn Kirk

From the Fasti[16] we learn that Andrew Dalrymple was married to Elizabeth Ross and had a daughter Margaret. He gained income from his Drumfork rentals, and presumably lived at the mansion house of Drumfork rather than the manse. He was minister of Auchinleck from 1651 until 1662 when, like many Ayrshire ministers, he was forced to leave his church by the Acts of Parliament and of the Privy Council. There was great unrest and many Scottish Presbyterian ministers lost their churches, refusing to have bishops and the Episcopalian church imposed on them by Charles II, and refusing to swear allegiance to him as head of the Church. Of course, Ayrshire was a stronghold of these Covenanters. In March 1669 he was accused of preaching and baptizing

16 *Registrum Fasti Ecclesiae Scoticanae* Vol.3 p3 & p67

irregularly, so although he had no church it appears that he was still ministering to his flock. He was indulged by the Privy Council in Sorn on the 2nd September 1669. By the Act of Indulgence, ousted ministers were allowed to return to their own Church if possible or an alternative one, so to Dalgain he returned and was minister there until his death in June 1676. He had been fined by the Privy Council on the 8th July 1673 for not keeping the 29th May which was the day of the Restoration of Charles II; his sympathies were certainly never with the king. He was buried at Auchinleck Kirk, his epitaph, translated from Latin, reads. 'Here lies a true follower of genuine piety, a favourer of honesty, an honour to religion, a distinguished pastor of Christ, 'who fed the flock' by his example, and by his words, which flowed like honey; of a peaceful disposition, second to none in integrity; the tomb holds his members, his mind flies beyond the stars.'[17] Even taking this with a large 'pinch of salt' he seems to have been one of the good guys.

The religious unrest during and after the 'Wars of the Three Kingdoms' would come to its bloodiest zenith during the 'Killing Times' of the 1680s and Ayrshire and the southwest of Scotland was at the forefront. Previously the Covenanters from the western counties between the Clyde and the Solway had formed a distinct administrative area known as the Western Association. They were extreme in their beliefs, even republican, and known as Remonstrants.[18] Andrew Dalrymple and his associates had strong covenanting principles. David Boswell of Auchinleck was summoned

17 Love, Dane, *The History of Auchinleck; Village and Parish*, p51

18 Haggart, Craig, *The Engagement; Theocracy; the last Anglo-Scots war; and the Commonwealth: Scotland 1648-60*, p4

before the Privy Council in 1678 and charged with attending field conventicles.[19] The local Mauchline minister, James Veitch, was imprisoned in 1662 for failing to take the Oath of Allegiance and then exiled to Holland in 1664 for refusing to lead the thanksgiving for Charles II's delivery from the Rye House Plot. He too, like Dalrymple, was fined in 1673 for failing to observe the king's birthday and in 1681 was put to the horn and his goods escheated as he 'rebelliously preached to the people the observance of the said Covenant.'[20]

To add to all this unrest, uncertainty and terror, troops were quartered in Mauchline and the surrounding area causing much hardship for the locals to whom they had to feed and give board.[21] John Reid of Daldilling, known for his cruelty and referred to as 'bloody Reid of Daldilling,'[22] was stationed with troops at Kingencleugh whilst Lauder with his dragoons was quartered at Sorn Castle.[23]

Amid all this unrest the legal wrangling and complex financial dealings regarding Drumfork continued. During the latter half of the seventeenth century Drumfork appears to be used as collateral for a series of bonds and debts.[24] The main 'players' were Robert Spottiswood minister at Crichton Church, Dumfriesshire, and William Reid of Daldilling. As debt passes to heirs, further generations are mentioned. Records show that there was an apprising between Andrew Dalrymple

---

19 Ducharme, Diane, *Guide to the Boswell Collection GEN MSS 89,* p11

20 Dennison, E Patricia; Gallagher, Dennis; Ewart, Gordon, *Historic Mauchline Archaeology and Development,* p26

21 Ibid. p27

22 Scottish Covenanter Memorials Association

23 Steven, Helen J., *Sorn Parish: Its History and Associations,* p21

24 Yale University, Beinecke Rare Book and Manuscript Library Boswell Collection GEN MSS 89 Series XV b.114, f 2066-69 Suits for debt

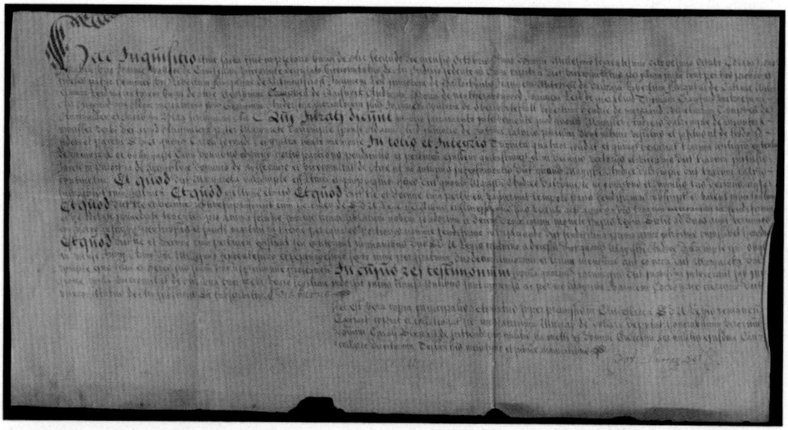

Fig. 20: Special Retour for Margaret Dalrymple, 1688.

and William Reid of Daldilling regarding Drumfork.[25] It has been difficult to check these records at length as copies are unobtainable. However, from studying Andrew Dalrymple's testaments, we see that this William Reid of Daldilling, a covenanting minister in Belliwalter, Ireland and Andrew Dalrymple, a covenanting minister at Auchinleck, are closely connected. One 'red herring' was the testament of an Adam Dalrymple of Drumfork, dated 1690.[26] Could he possibly be a brother to Andrew? However, since there is no mention of an Adam Dalrymple either in the Fasti or as a minister at Sorn Church and Adam is not a Dalrymple family name, we must assume that it is a clerical error, especially when much of the Testament mentions Adam Aird. This 1690 Testament is a later one for Andrew Dalrymple, his first testament is dated 1676.[27] It certainly appears rather unusual to have two

25 National Records of Scotland GD253/136
26 National Records of Scotland CC9/7/47/425-6
27 National Records of Scotland CC9/7/41

testaments!

Even with all the dispute and legal wrangling, Andrew's daughter, Margaret Dalrymple, would inherit Drumfork and her Retour of Heir is dated 2nd October 1688.[28] 'Margaret Dalrymple spouse of Adam Aird junior of Catrine, heir of magistri Andrew Dalrymple of Drumfork, minister of the word of God at Auchinleck, father, 34 shilling and 5 pence land of auld extent of Drumfork and Ballangape cum decimus, in parish of Mauchline, et domino Kylesmuir' The names mentioned in the above document were presumably her relations and kin group, and reads like a 'who's who' of those who had wealth and influence in the locality: Robert Farquhar of Gilmilnscroft (possibly her uncle), John Reid junior of Ballochmyle, John Mitchell of Dalgain, Robert Farquhar of Catrine, William Reid merchant and burgess in Ayr, George Campbell of Glaisnock, Andrew Brown of Netherwellwood, John Reid of Merkland, Thomas Crawford heritor in Ayr, Alexander Adair merchant in Ayr, George Anderson merchant in Ayr, John Wilson of Overwhiteflat, Robert Hendry of Merkland, William Campbell of Auchmillan, James Blair(?) in Ayr.

A year previously on 16th June 1687 she had married Adam Aird junior of Catrine.[29] A vast amount of information can be gleaned from their marriage contract. It was drawn up at Drumfork on the 14th of April 1687 and is a fascinating legal document covering every eventuality of the marriage. If Margaret or Adam were to die, if there were no heirs, if there were only female heirs, if either of them remarries etc. It also

28 Retours of Services of Heirs 653

29 Yale University, Beinecke Rare Book and Manuscript Library Boswell Collection GEN MSS 89 Series XV b.114, f 2070 Marriage contract: Margaret Dalrymple and Adam Aird of Catrine

goes into detail about who was to gain liferents of Drumfork, notably Elizabeth Ross, and mentions some of the local gentry and those with a financial interest. From this we learn that Andrew Dalrymple's first wife was Agnes Farquhar and she, not Elizabeth Ross, was the mother of Margaret. Margaret was probably born about 1667 as she inherited Drumfork in 1688. Possibly Andrew's second wife, Elizabeth Ross, was the younger sister of Margaret Ross of Balneill, wife of James Dalrymple, first earl of Stair. On 22nd September 1651 Robert Farquhar of Gilmilnscroft had married Elizabeth, daughter of James Ross of Balneill in Wigtownshire, her tocher was 8000 merks. The witnesses were James Dalrymple of Stair, John McDowall, and Alexander Bailes.[30] We learn that Robert Farquhar died in 1670.[31] Would Robert Farquhar be the brother or a close connection to Andrew Dalrymple's first wife Agnes Farquhar?

To have the survival of Margaret Dalrymple and Adam Aird's marriage contract is amazing. The marriage contracts of Mungo Reid and Margaret Farquhar and of Mungo Reid and Isobell Boswell would have, no doubt, followed a similar format and it is a pity that they have not survived.

One can imagine the excitement as Margaret's wedding day draws near, the paperwork finalised, preparations made, the food, the drink the guests, possibly the wedding took place at Drumfork. She then moves into the 'new house' Nether Catrine House, a fine example of a laird's house, situated at the bottom of Townhead Street in Catrine and built for Adam Aird's father.[32] It has the inscription AA and HR with the

30 Paterson, James, *A History of the County of Ayr*, Vol.2 p699

31 *Burke Genealogical & Heraldic History of Great Britain* Vol 3 Online

32 www.ayrshirehistory.com/catrine

Fig. 21: Nether Catrine House

date of 1682 which would be Adam Aird and his wife Hellen Reid. It is now flats and the better view is from the back but thankfully it has survived.

Unfortunately, Margaret like her mother Agnes Farquhar was to die young, most probably in childbirth or thereabouts as there is a child, Adam Aird. A discharge of debt document[33] and Andrew Dalrymple's second testament shows that she is dead by 1689. In 1688 when she inherits Drumfork she is pregnant with her first child and the following year is no more, childbirth, perilous for all women both the high-born and the poor.

> 'The start of her lying-in was the end of mornings……
> Birth the leveller pays no heed to class, to kind – ' [34]

33 Yale University, Beinecke Rare Book and Manuscript Library Boswell Collection GEN MSS 89 Series XV b.114, f 2071-73 Inheritance of Margaret Dalrymple

34 Meehan, Paula 'This Bed, This Raft on Stormy Seas to Melpomene –

In 1696 Adam Aird married a Jean Dunbar. Adam, his son from his first marriage probably died as there is no mention of him in later documents, only his children with his second wife. One of their daughters, Christian, married an Archibald Stewart, Writer to the Signet in Edinburgh, and he bought Catrine House from her father. The estate stayed with the Stewart family for many years, and they used it as their 'holiday home' escaping the city to the beautiful Ayrshire countryside. There is a lovely description of the house in a book about Dugald Stewart, Chair of Moral Philosophy at Edinburgh University.[35] 'The old mansion house of Catrine (built 1682) stands on the left bank of the water of Ayr, in a picturesque and well wooded valley. It continued to be a favourite summer retreat of Mr Stewart for many years after his appointment to the Chair at the University. Its charms for him as a residence were, however, destroyed by the erection in 1792 of a large cotton mill on the opposite bank of the river, and the consequent rise, in room of the small and secluded hamlet of Catrine, of a populous manufacturing village.'

And a short distance from the planned village of Catrine is Drumfork.

In 1714 Adam Aird sold Drumfork to James Boswell of Auchinleck, the seventh laird and grandfather of James Boswell the diarist.[36] This was Boswell's first major purchase as he was expanding his land holding.[37] Drumfork was to remain part of the Auchinleck estate until after World War 1.

Muse of Tragedy'

35 Stewart, Dugald, *The Collected works of Dugald Stewart*, p xiii

36 National Records of Scotland RS 14-7-2-00002

37 Ducharme, Diane, *Guide to the Boswell Collection GEN MSS 89.* p22

7

Drumfork; Some Tenants

Little evidence has survived of the tenants who lived and worked the lands of Drumfork. There is, however, one notorious snapshot of tenant life from the Mauchline Kirk Session records of 1673, giving an account of a drink fuelled row at Drumfork.[1] There are allegations of witchcraft which could have taken a more serious turn, especially in the seventeenth century context with witch trials widespread and executions not uncommon. Notary Andrew Dalrymple was reputedly on the Assise at the Janet Smeallie witch trial in Ayr in 1630[2] and the last mass execution for witchcraft was in nearby Paisley in 1697.[3]

In May 1673 Drumfork tenants Isobell Boswell, the 'gudewife of Drumfork,' and her daughter Marion Reid, along with John Reid and Janet (*Jonet*) Reid, are called before the Kirk Session on charges of scolding, cursing and fighting. The Kirk Session held great sway over the lives and morals of the population of Mauchline and could interfere in all aspects of life. People were called before them for all manner of misdemeanours, think of Robert Burns in the following century. It would appear that this is Isobell Boswell, wife or possibly now widow, of Mungo Reid (4) the last of the Reid lairds. They may have fallen on hard times but at least they

1 Paterson, James, *A History of the County of Ayr,* Vol.2 p328

2 Shearer, Joseph D., *Ayr and its People,* p82

3 Adam, Isabel, *Witch Hunt; the great Scottish Witchcraft Trials of 1697.*

could still afford their wine, and plenty of it!

This really was quite a stramash, Marion Reid was accused of fighting, scolding, and using obscene language and abusing Janet Reid, Adam Reid's sister. Seemingly these two ladies already had 'form' as there had been an earlier accusation by Marion that Janet had taken a sey apron off the dyke and was 'a common thief.' All of them were the worse for drink and Marion Reid claimed that Janet had drunk five mutchkins of wine, a mutchkin being about three quarters of an imperial pint.[4] Isobell Boswell was charged with scolding and beating John Reid and admitted to calling him a 'witch-get'. John Reid is charged with drunkenness and calling the 'gudewife of Drumfork', a 'whoore and a witch'. He agreed that he had called her a 'liar like a witch' and a 'whoore' but only after she had called him a 'witch-get'. Having been called twice, Janet Reid failed to appear at the Kirk Session. However, witnesses were called and under oath made the following comments: Matthew Baird said that he heard Marion Reid call Janet Reid a 'thief.' George Bowie said that John Reid had 'danced in his own house' and had called Marion Reid a 'drunken limmer.' James Wood said that he heard the 'gudewife of Drumfork' call John Reid 'witch-get' and heard him call her a 'liar like a witch.' Jean Campbell said that she thought both the 'gudewife of Drumfork' and John Reid drunk (rather an understatement), and she had called him 'a witches get' and he had said that she 'lied like a witch'. Janet Reid finally attended the Kirk Session at the end of June and was charged with calling Marion Reid a thief and scolding. This dispute finally ended with the Kirk Session ordering the four of them to be publicly rebuked on a Sabbath day. We can visualize this altercation and perhaps

4 Oxford Dictionary Online

smile at the antics and feel the world has changed little in four hundred years. Indeed, some would regard this as a typical Ayrshire night out. Oh, to have been a fly on the wall!

The names Lennox, Henry, Pedin, Murdoch and Wilson have already been mentioned and from the 'Boswell Book' we know these names continue into the eighteenth century and doubtless beyond.[5]

From a Disposition of 1669[6] we know that the Pedins (*Paithines*) farmed at Drumfork Mains. Thomas Pedin's testament[7] shows that he was a tenant from 1664 until his death in 1674 and had previously farmed at Heateth, often referred to as Pedin's Heateth. After his wife, Elizabeth Smith, died in 1659 he joined his son-in-law, John Wilson, along the road in Drumfork Mains, an extended family in the one household, a dutiful daughter taking care of her elderly father. Also mentioned is his grey horse worth £24, two heifers worth 53/4d, corn with an estimated value of £22/10s and the same estimate for his barley. He had two cartloads of hay valued at 8/4d and the contents of his house and his clothing valued at £8, his total worth was £65/3/4d. Unfortunately, he owed rent of £72, being five bolls of meal and one of barley at £12 per boll, to Andrew Dalrymple, minister at Dalgain, his debts, therefore, exceeded the value of his goods.

Thomas Pedin's testament also shows a Bond of Caution between Ninian Dougall in Hall of Gilmilnscroft

5 Hankins, N. P., & Strawhorn, J. (Editors), *The Correspondence of James Boswell with James Bruce and Andrew Gibb, Overseers of the Auchinleck Estate*

6 Yale University, Beinecke Rare Book and Manuscript Library Boswell Collection GEN MSS 89 Series XV b.114, f 2065 Disposition of the lands of Drumfork and Ballangape to Andrew Dalrymple 1669

7 National Records of Scotland CC/9/7/40

and John Wilson in Drumfork. Possibly the same Ninian Dougall, a tailor from Gilmilnscroft, who appears on a list of prisoners from the battle of Bothwell Brig?[8] On 22nd June 1679, after victory at Drumclog, the Covenanters were defeated by Government forces under the command of the Duke of Monmouth and Viscount Dundee at Bothwell Brig. Covenanters deaths were about 600 to 700, and some 1200 were taken prisoner and marched to imprisonment in Greyfriars Kirkyard, Edinburgh.[9] While some were executed and others sent to the Colonies, many were released if they swore not to join future conventicles. Ninian Dougall did this, however, his excuse for being in the vicinity of the battle is genius denying that he was fighting there and saying that he just happened to be in the area visiting his wife's cousin! A deposition before the Privy Council of 30th June 1679 states, 'Ninian Dougall taylor in Gilmilnscroft married confesses he joined with the rebells the day before ther defate and came only to see a cusine of his wyffs and hade no armes declaires he wes never at three conventicles and if he wer at libertie he should goe no more.' On 9th July he was given a travel pass to return to Ayrshire.[10]

Elizabeth Smith's Testament of 1664 gives a snapshot of the size of Heateth. She had died there in 1659 and again her son in law, John Wilson, was executor. She and her husband had three bolls of corn valued at £4 each, a cow worth £12 and two young bullocks together worth £4 and the contents of the house and her clothing came to £13/6/8d. She owed £16 duty to James Pedin (*Paiden*) in the waulkmill, and her cautioner

8 'Find My Past' Scottish Covenanters 1679- 1688 JC39/19

9 Battle of Bothwell bridge www.battlefieldstrust.com

10 'Find My Past' Scottish Covenanters 1679- 1688 JC39/19

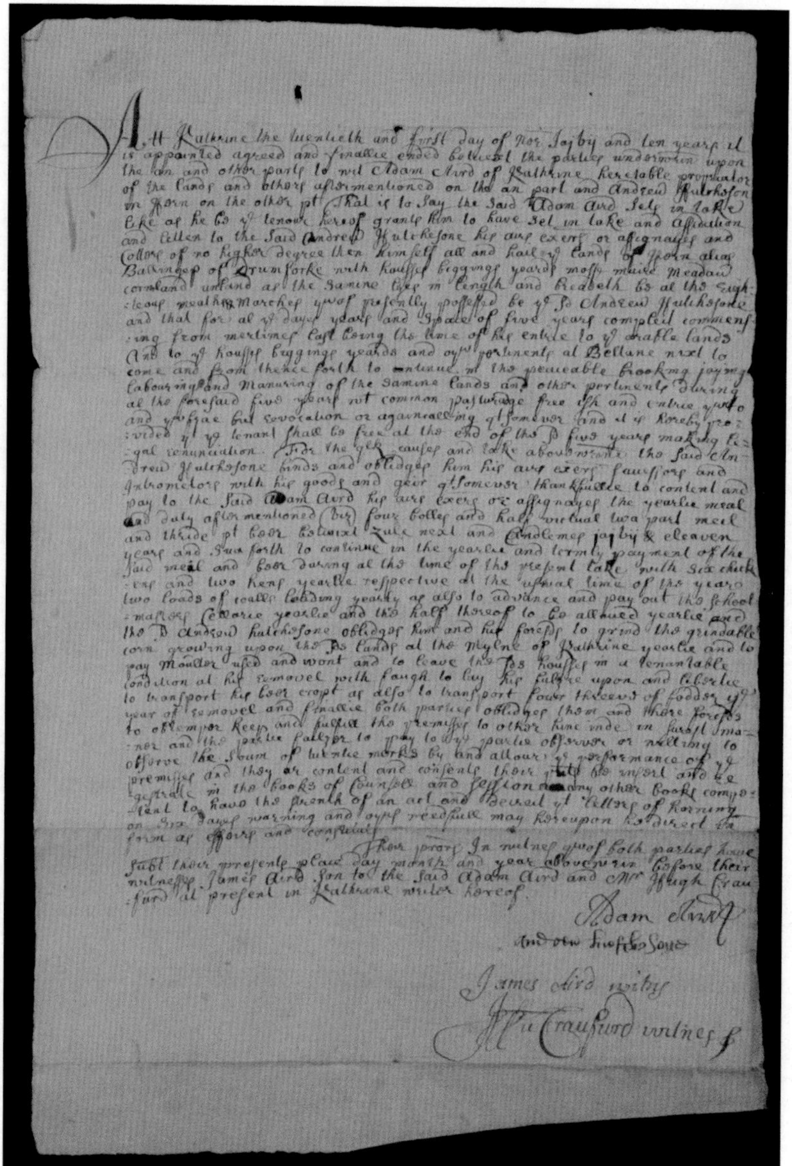

At Kathrine the twentieth and first day of Nov. [illegible] and ten years it is appointed agreed and finallie ended betwixt the parties underwritten upon the ane and other parts to wit Adam Aird of Kathrine heretable proprietor of the lands and others aftermentioned on the ane part and Andrew Hutcheson in Hern on the other pt. That is to say the said Adam Aird sets in tack like as he be yr tenour hereof grants him to have set in tack and assedation and letten to the said Andrew Hutchesone his airs exers or assignayes and collors of no higher degree then himself all and haill yr lands of Hern alias Ballingap of Drumforke with housses biggings yeards moss muire meadow cornland [illegible] as the samine lyes in length and breadth be al the eight [illegible] marches ywof presently possessed be ye sd Andrew Hutchesone and that for al ye dayes years and space of five years compleit commensing from mertimes last being the tyme of his entrie to ye arable lands And to ye housses biggings yeards and oyr pertinents at Beltane next to come and from thence forth to continue in the peaceable brooking joying labouring and manuring of the samine lands and other pertinents during al the foresaid five years wt common pasturage free ish and entrie ywto and ywfrae but revocation or againcalling qtsomever and it is hereby provided yt ye tenant shall be free at the end of the sd five years making legal renunciation. For the qlk causes and tack abovewritten the said Andrew Hutchesone binds and obliedges him his airs exers [illegible] and [illegible] with his goods and geir qtsomever thankfullie to content and pay to the said Adam Aird his airs exers or assignayes the yearlie meal and duty aftermentioned viz four bolles and half victual two part meal and thride pt beer betwixt Zule next and Candlemes [illegible] & eleaven years and sua forth to continue in the yearlie and termly payment of the said meal and beer during al the time of the present tack with six chickens and two hens yearlie respective at the usual time of the yeare two loads of coalls leading yearly as also to advance and pay out the school masters sellarie yearlie and the half thereof to be allowed yearlie and the sd Andrew Hutchesone obliedges him and his forcess to grind the grindable corn growing upon the sd lands at the mylne of Kathrine yearlie and to pay moulter used and wont and to leave the sd housses in a tenantable condition at his removel with faugh to lay his fullzie upon and liberlie to transport his beer cropt as also to transport fower threeves of fodder ye year of removel and finallie both parties obliedges them and there forcess to observe keep and fulfill the premisses to other hine inde in lawful manner and the partie failzer to pay to ye partie observer or willing to observe the soum of twentie merks by and attour ye performance of ye premisses and they ar content and consents thir ptts be insert and registrate in the books of Counsell and Session or any other books competent to have the strenth of an act and decreit yt letters of horning on six dayes warning and oyrs needfull may hereupon be direct in form as effeirs and constitute [illegible] their prors. In witness ywof both parties have subt their presents place day month and year abovewritten before their witnesses James Aird son to the said Adam Aird and Mr Hugh Craufurd at present in Kathrine writer hereof.

Adam Aird

Andrew Hutchesone

James Aird witnes

Hu Craufurd witnes

Fig. 22: Tack of Hern alias Ballangape of Drumfork, 1710.

was William Barry in Logan. The waulkmill referred to may well be the waulkmill of Sorn, west of Sorn castle by the river Ayr. In 1684 two fugitives held in the parish were Robert Pedin and his brother, (name unknown) sons to Hugh Pedin in the waulkmill of Sorn.[11]

It is interesting to note that 50 years previously in the 1625 Sasine of Brackenhill, we have witnesses John Pedin (*Pathene*) in Nether Heateth and Robert Wilson in Drumfork, possibly forbears of Thomas Pedin and his son-in-law John Wilson.

In the charter for the sale of Hern in 1626[12] we have mention of a Charles Murdoch in Drumfork as a witness, a wee glimpse of another tenant family.

Some tacks still survive from this period giving a fascinating glimpse of life at Drumfork.

A tack of 1710[13] is for Hern alias Ballangape of Drumfork drawn up between Adam Aird, of Catrine 'heritable proprietor' of the land and Andrew Hutchison in Hern. The format is typical of a tack of its time and includes the usual terminology of 'houses, biggings, yards, mosses, muir, meadow, cornland and upland.' It is for five years with access to the arable land from Martinmas and entry to the house from Beltane. It then details what is expected of Hutchison in 'brooking, joining, labouring and manuring the ground'. He is to pay yearly meal of four and a half bolles victual, two-part meal and the third part bere, as well as six chickens,

11 Jardine's Book of Martyrs drjardine.wordpress.com/2016/09/26/prophet-pedens-kinsfolk-history-scotland/

12 National Records of Scotland RS12/4/378

13 Yale University, Beinecke Rare Book and Manuscript Library Boswell Collection GEN MSS 89 Series XV b.114, f 2075 Tacks of Drumfork by Aird

two hens, two loads of coal at certain time of the year and payment towards the schoolmaster's fee. He is to use the mill at Catrine. Hutchison was to leave the place in a 'tenantable' condition when the tack ended. It was signed by Adam Aird and Andrew Hutchison and witnessed by James Aird, Adam Aird's son and John Crawford.

An earlier tenant of Ballangape was a William Richardson (*Rechertson*) living there in 1564,[14] another tantalising glimpse of an Ayrshire family.

A tack of 1712[15] between Adam Aird and John Livingstone does not say which part of Drumfork it applies to other than the ground occupied by John Parker. It appears that a person's name would be enough to indicate which parcel of land was being referred to. It was to be for nine years with entry to the arable land at Martinmas and the house and yards at Beltane. Livingstone is to pay Aird 'nine bolls of good and sufficient oatmeal' between Yule and Candlemas and two bolls of bere at Beltane as well as twenty-five pounds Scots silver at Beltane with two hens in January and six chickens at the usual time as well as eight loads of coal when required. This is for the first two years and then for the next two years he is to pay one boll of meal more. He too is obliged to use the Mill at Catrine and pay towards the schoolmaster's salary. John Aird, Adam's brother, is a witness to this document as is Hugh Pedin (*Pethin*) in Croftfoot and George Hunter in Daldorch. The eight loads of coal for this parcel of Drumfork indicates that this was a larger holding than Ballangape of

14 Yale University, Beinecke Rare Book and Manuscript Library Boswell Collection GEN MSS 89 Series XV oversize b.129 f.2380

15 Yale University, Beinecke Rare Book and Manuscript Library Boswell Collection GEN MSS 89 Series XV b.114, f 2075 Tacks of Drumfork by Aird

Drumfork which only required two loads of coal.

We note that one hundred and fifty years earlier a John Livingstone (*Johne Levingstone*) was a tenant in Whirr (*Calzeqhuoir*), surely a forebear of the above John Livingstone?[16]

A third surviving tack is of Gulzie Mailing or as it is written Goollymealing.[17] This tack, written at Mauchline and dated the fifteenth of February 1713 is between Adam Aird and Andrew Millar. It indicates that Gulzie Mailing is in Mauchline parish. It follows the usual format of entry to the land at Martinmas and the house and yards at Beltane. He is to pay five merks of money rent yearly as well as 'five bolls of good and sufficient oatmeal' between Yule and Candlemas and five chickens at Lammas every year. Again, two loads of coal when required and payment towards the schoolmaster's salary and Catrine Mill was to be used. It was signed by Adam Aird and witnessed by John Campbell in Kingencleugh and Robert Millar, merchant in Mauchline. A later 1736 Tack of Gulzie Mailing between James Boswell and Hugh Pedin gives lovely descriptions of the extent of the farm and detailed instructions of how it is to be farmed.

We must remember that these tenants were farming a pre-enclosure landscape of small scattered fermtouns with their infield and outfield and communal working practices, and the countryside would look radically different to today.

A copy of a letter from James Boswell to Robert Reid in Drumfork (he was in Drumfork Mains, the names appearing

16 Yale University, Beinecke Rare Book and Manuscript Library Boswell Collection GEN MSS 89 Series XV oversize b.129 f.2380

17 Yale University, Beinecke Rare Book and Manuscript Library Boswell Collection GEN MSS 89 Series XV b.114, f 2077 Tacks of Drumfork by Aird

to be interchangeable by the eighteenth century) survives giving an insight into the farm on the cusp of enclosure.[18] It was written in London on 11th December 1790, and follows the standard format of a tack. Basically, Boswell wishes Robert (first name terms here) to continue farming Drumfork and offers to lime a third of the farm and enclose it into nine parks. Obviously for these improvements there is to be a progressive rent, nine shillings per acre for the first three years of an eighteen-year lease, eleven shillings the next three years and thirteen shillings for the remaining years. Seemingly this rent is a shilling per acre less than Boswell would ask from a stranger. There is then a direction as to what should and should not be ploughed. It is fascinating to learn that bees were kept at Drumfork as Robert Reid was to pay 'one pint of virgin honey yearly'. He was to increase the number of loads of coal that was to be carried to 'the place,' one assumes Auchinleck House and to pay double the number of hens and chickens than he currently did. Boswell also promises to 'enclose the road through your farm without delay.' Boswell feels he has made a kindly offer, and he means to 'encourage' Robert Reid to continue his lease of the farm.

This letter is fantastic evidence of enclosure, possibly all the farms on the Auchinleck Estate were being enclosed at this time. Does the hedging and fencing which exists today on what was Drumfork Mains reflect some of this original enclosure? Again, it is fascinating to learn that the road through the farm to Mauchline dates from the 1790s and no doubt the 'road to nowhere' was enclosed then too. It is hard to visualise the pre-enclosure landscape as we are so used to fields and hedge. In a fifty year span the countryside

18 National Records of Scotland GD1/1278/8

was totally transformed, and then further changed with the advent of the railways.

These tenants, and the others whose names and existence we do not know, lived, and died in one small area and we can only glimpse their lives. The daily grind of eking out an existence from the land, their drinking, dancing and arguing with neighbours, their joys, and sorrows. Yet they and their forebears rode out to battle with their laird, joined in skirmishes, and took to the hills to worship their God.

Beyond 1714

By 1714 most of the lands of Drumfork were part of the Auchinleck estate, other than Whirr and Gulzie Mailing, both of which were included by the end of the eighteenth century. There are many more surviving records from 1700. However, a detailed history is for another day.

Thomas Guthrie followed by his son, another Thomas, farmed Drumfork for much of the eighteenth century whilst Robert Reid was at Drumfork Mains. The Mains seemed to have been incorporated into Drumfork in the early nineteenth century and was certainly gone by the 1841 census. For most of the nineteenth century the Bryson family were tenants. After the First World War many of the estate farms were sold off and Drumfork was purchased by the Mairs who farmed there for several generations. By 2000 there was a quick succession of owners the Stirrats, the Pattersons, and presently the Hills.

Over the years Drumfork saw the Reids as kindly tenants, feuars and possibly tenants again, followed by the Dalrymples and Airds as landowners. However, below their level there were so many people living off the land, so many names lost to history.

This has been a fascinating story to tell of Drumfork, a small two hundred acre farm. Multiply this by every farm in the district and a gripping local history enfolds, our history, our ancestors, our Ayrshire.

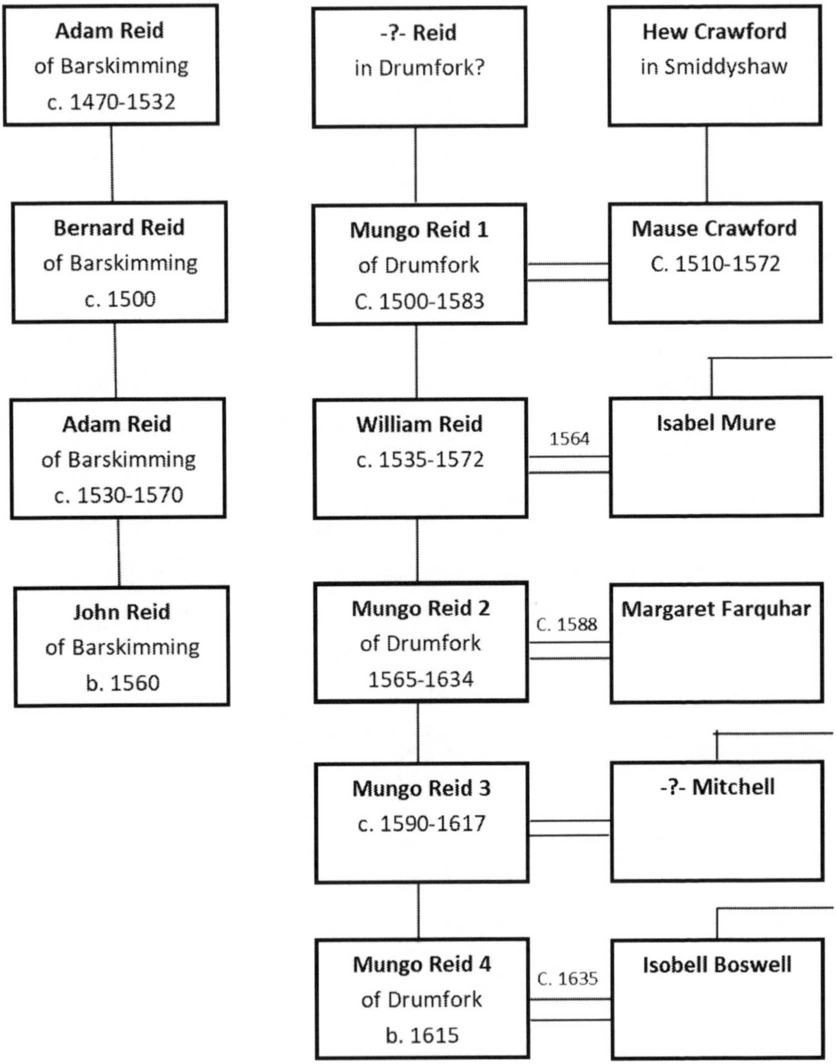
Adam Reid
of Barskimming
c. 1470-1532
-?- Reid
in Drumfork?
Hew Crawford
in Smiddyshaw
Bernard Reid
of Barskimming
c. 1500
Mungo Reid 1
of Drumfork
C. 1500-1583
Mause Crawford
C. 1510-1572
Adam Reid
of Barskimming
c. 1530-1570
William Reid
c. 1535-1572
1564
Isabel Mure
John Reid
of Barskimming
b. 1560
Mungo Reid 2
of Drumfork
1565-1634
C. 1588
Margaret Farquhar
Mungo Reid 3
c. 1590-1617
-?- Mitchell
Mungo Reid 4
of Drumfork
b. 1615
C. 1635
Isobell Boswell

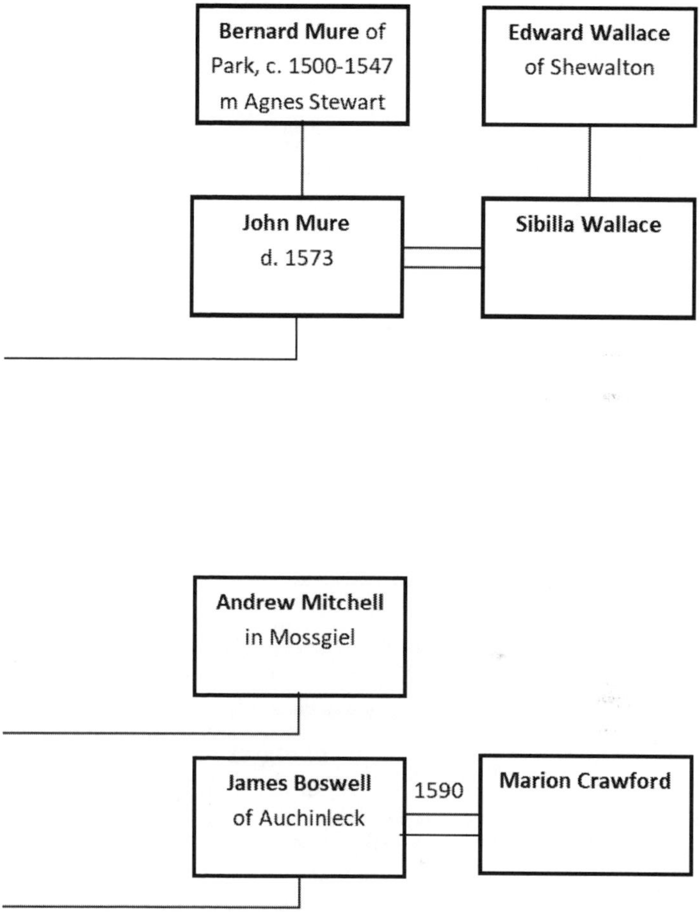

Reid Family Tree

Glossary

Alienation -Transference of ownership (especially land).

Apprising - The valuation of estimated worth, often of land to pay debts. Also, the sentence of a sheriff by which heritable rights belonging to the debtor were sold for payment of the debt due to the appriser.

Arriage and Carriage - A term used to signify services by horses, or carriage by horses, due by a tenant to his landlord.

Assise – A judicial inquiry by a number of people appointed for that purpose; the body of persons so appointed.

Baillie – A representative appointed to carry out a specific function, usually the giving of sasine.

Bairn's Part - share of a father's free moveable property on which the father's death the children are entitled to.

Bastle House – Generally a two-storey fortified farmhouse with living accommodation on the first floor and shelter for cattle and sheep on the ground floor.

Beltane - May 1st, May Day.

Bere - A kind of barley hardier than the ordinary kind but of inferior quality.

Boll - A measure of capacity for grain, malt, salt etc.

Bond - A written obligation to pay or perform something.

Bondage Silver - service at harvest commuted to a monetary fee.

Bonnet Laird - A small landowner (wore a bonnet not the hat of the gentry).

Burgess - Person having the freedom of a burgh.

Candlemas - February 2nd.

Caution - Security, bail.

Cautioner - The person who becomes security, a surety.

Chalmer - chamber.

Charter - An instrument of disposition in the form of a letter, usually the donation or gift of property or the granting of legal rights.

Clare Constat - Name of a precept (an order) in which a superior acknowledges that it 'clearly appears' that someone is heir to landed property held of the superior, and which orders the giving of sasine.

Crown Remission - The formal pardon for an offence.

Curator - An administrator of another person's affairs either nominated in a will or otherwise or appointed by court, often of a minor aged over 12 for boys and 14 for girls.

Deposition - The testimony of a witness put down in writing.

Dispone - To transfer legal ownership.

Escheat - Property, possessions, or goods taken from a person by forfeiture or confiscation, especially falling to the crown in this way.

Feu - Feudal holding, land granted to the Vassal by his Superior in return for feu-duty (cash or kind).

Feu Farm - A type of land ownership where the owner pays a yearly fee called 'feu duty' in exchange for the right to use the land.

Gudewife - Mistress of a household, farm.

Guids and Gear – Possessions (moveable as opposed to heritable).

Horning, letters of - a letter in the monarch's name whereby someone is charged for defaulting on an agreement or to pay or perform what had been agreed within a set time under pain of being denounced rebel and 'put to the horn', opening the way for the defaulters' moveables to be escheat to the Crown.

Husbandland - A division of land occupied originally by a husband or tenant of a manor, most common in north England and southeast Scotland, obsolete c.1600. It appears to have been equal to 2 bovates or ox-gangs, about 26 acres.

Infeft - To invest with legal possession a person with heritable property.

Kindly Tenant - They held their tenancies for a low or 'favourable' rent. Unlike normal tenants, it was understood that they could be succeeded in their holdings by their heirs.

Ky - cattle.

Liferent - A right to receive until death the revenue of a property without the right to dispose of the capital.

Mail - Rent, chiefly as paid in money as opposed to kind.

Mains - The home farm of an estate, usually worked by the proprietor but sometimes leased to tenants.

Martinmas - November 11th, feast of St Martin.

Mell(with) - Have dealings with (used in a testament, it applies to the executor's disposal of the deceased's property).

Merk - Currency with the value of approximately two thirds of one-pound Scots or 12 shillings and 4 pence. A silver coin of this denomination was coined at intervals from the reign of James VI in 1578 to that of Charles II.

Multure - The duty, consisting of a proportion of the grain, extracted by the proprietor or tenant of a mill on all corn ground there.

Mutchkin - A Scots pint equivalent to four gills, 0.43 litres.

Notary Public - A lawyer or official charged with authenticating documents and transactions.

Officer - One employed in an official capacity, often in Customs or local administration.

Old Extent - Names give to the valuation of land during the reign of Alexander III.

Park - An enclosure, not necessarily ornamental, for animals, grass or crops.

Perambulator - A person who has walked round the boundaries of a certain lands to verify them and is mentioned in a charter as performing this act of 'perambulation', the official in charge of this process.

Petaries - A place where peat is excavated.

Portioner - The proprietor of a small estate or piece of land resulting from the division of an original forty merkland among co-heirs or otherwise, a small landowner.

Procuratory of Resignation - The authority granted by a vassal to his representative (who in this case called his procurator) to restore the lands held by a vassal to his superior, either to remain in the superior's hands or to be granted out again.

Quartermaster - Organiser of supplies, usually in the army or in a guild.

Resignation - This occurred when a vassal gave up his estate to the superior, either permanently or 'in favorem,' i.e., where the intention was that the superior should make a new grant in favour of another, usually a purchaser from the person resigning the land.

Sasine - The act or procedure of giving possession of feudal property, by the symbolic delivery of earth and stones or similar appropriate objects on the property itself.

Scolding - Violent, verbal abuse.

Service of Heirs - On the death of a landowner, the heir had to prove his right to inherit the land. An investigation took place to ascertain the extent of the land held by the deceased, and a retour (return) of the jury's decision was made to the Chancery. The heir received a copy of the retour, thereby ratifying the entitlement.

Servitor - An assistant, lawyer's clerk, apprentice, assistant schoolmaster.

Sey - A kind of woollen cloth, resembling serge.

SHERIFF - A non-hereditary official in charge of a shire who carried out administrative duties.

SLAUGHTER - Public killing.

SUPERIOR - A granter of land to another, who becomes his vassal in return for perpetual payment of feu-duty.

SUPPLY, COMMISSIONERS OF - Persons who were nominated every year in each county, to levy the land tax due from their county, maintain roads and control the raising of militia etc.

TACK - A lease, tenancy, especially the leasehold tenure of a farm, mill, mining, or fishing rights.

TENANT - One who holds the land (generally for a fixed term) by a lease or tack.

TENEMENT - In legal terms a landholding, usually (but not always) a piece of land which is built upon.

TESTAMENT - A written deed appointing an executor to administer a person's moveable property after his death.

THIRLAGE - Astriction or thirlage to a mill, the obligation imposed on tenants of having the grain from their lands ground at a particular mill.

TOCHER - Marriage portion, dowry paid by a bride's family, chiefly her father, to the groom or his family, usually paid a year and a day after the marriage.

Turbaries - A place where turf or peat is dug.

Tutor - A person who is guardian and administrator of the estate of a pupil or child under the age of 12 if female and 14 if male. In land, an administrator over such a property on behalf of a minor. Differs from a curator by having responsibility for the child's person in addition to their estate.

Vassal - One who has the exclusive possession and use of land in perpetuity in return for a fixed annual payment of feu-duty to a superior.

Wadset - A written deed which transferred land to another as security for, or in satisfaction of, a debt due to him by the granter (called the reverser) to redeem his lands from the lender of the money (called the wadsetter) when his debt was repaid, or his obligation fulfilled.

Wappenschaw - A 'show of weapons', the periodical muster or review of the able-bodied men in a particular lordship or district to prove that they had suitable arms and were (reasonably) competent in their use.

Warrandice - A guarantee as an undertaking to protect another, safe-keeping; or as given by a seller to buyer, vouching for the article sold.

Waulkmill - A fulling mill where cloth is made thick and felted by a process of soaking, beating and shrinking.

Witch-get - son of a witch.

Yule - December 21st Winter solstice.

TIMELINE

1503	Marriage of James IV and Margaret Tudor.
1513	Battle of Flodden and death of James IV, leading nobles and 'ordinary' men.
1513 - 1528	Minority of James V.
1526	Battle of Linlithgow Bridge.
1528	Siege of Tantallon.
1528 - 1542	Personal reign of James V.
1542	Battle of Solway Moss, death of James V, birth of Mary Queen of Scots.
1542 – 1561	Minority of Mary Queen of Scots.
1546	George Wishart burned for heresy and Cardinal Beaton assassinated.
1547	Battle of Pinkie.
1560	Protestant Reformation.
1561	Mary Queen of Scots returns to Scotland after death of her husband, Francis II of France.
1566	Birth of James VI.
1567	Deposition of Mary Queen of Scots.
1567 - 1573	Marian Civil War.
1579	Lairds ordered to have a Bible and Psalm Book in their houses.
1587	Execution of Mary Queen of Scots.
1603	Union of the Crowns.

1617	James VI returns to Scotland for a brief visit.
1625	Death of James VI and accession of Charles I.
1637 – 1651	Covenanter government in Scotland.
1638	Signing of the National Covenant.
1643	Signing of the Solemn League and Covenant.
1639 – 1653	War of the Three Kingdoms.
1648	Skirmish at Mauchline Muir.
1649	Execution of Charles I.
1650	Battle of Dunbar.
1651 - 1660	Cromwellian Occupation.
1660	Restoration of Charles II.
1661	Bishops restored to the Church of Scotland.
1663	The non-conforming ministers are expelled, increase in numbers of conventicles.
1679	Battles of Drumclog and Bothwell Brig.
1685	Death of Charles II and accession of James VII.
1681	Test Act.
1680 – 1688	'The Killing Times'.
1689	Accession of William and Mary.
1702	Death of William II and accession of Queen Anne.
1707	Union of the Parliaments.

Sources and Bibliography

Adam, Isabel, *Witch Hunt; the great Scottish Witchcraft trials of 1697*, London, 1978.

Anderson, Rev. John, *Calendar of the Laing Charters AD 854 - 1837*, Edinburgh, 1899.

Anderson, Rev. John; Grant, Francis J., *Protocol Book of Gavin Ros 1512 - 1532,* Edinburgh, 1908.

Baptie, Diane, *A Lairdship Lost: The Mowats of Balquholly 1309 - 1736,* East Linton, 2000.

Boswell J. J., *History and Genealogical Tables of the Boswells: Their Ancient Alliances and Connections from the founder of the Name in the year 1066, to this Date, 1906*, Scotland 1906.

Brown, Keith, *Bloodfeud in Scotland 1573 - 1625*, Edinburgh, 1986.

Dennison, E. Patricia; Gallagher, Dennis; Ewart, Gordon, *Historic Mauchline Archaeology and Development,* Edinburgh, 2006.

Devine, T. M., *Scotland's Empire 1600 - 1815*, London, 2003.

Dillon, W. J., *Origins of Feudal Ayrshire*, AANHS Collections, 2nd Series, Vol.3, 1955.

Ducharme, Diane J., *Guide to the Boswell Collection GEN MSS 89, Yale University Library,* Beinecke Rare Book and Manuscript Library, Yale, 1988.

Dumfries & Galloway Natural History & Antiquarian Society Third Series, Vol xxiv.

Duncan, A. A. M., *Scotland the Making of the Kingdom,* Edinburgh, 1978.

Easson, D.E., *Medieval Religious Houses in Scotland,* London, 1957.

Edmonstone, Sir Archibald, *Genealogical Account of the Family of Edmonstone of Duntreath*, Edinburgh, 1851.

Fergusson, Sir James, *Lowland Lairds - The Kilkerran Collection,* London, 1949.

Fergusson, Sir James, *The Ayrshire Casualties at Pinkie,* London, 1963.

Fondazione Sella, Biella

Fraser, Sir William, I*ntroductions and illustrations of the Annandale Family Book of the Johnstones, Earls and Marquises of Annandale*, Edinburgh, 1894.

Grant, Francis J. (Editor), *The Commissariot Record of Edinburgh. Register of Testaments.* Part 1, Vols.1-35, 1514 –

1600, Edinburgh, 1897.

Greig, Andrew, *Rose Nicolson*, London, 2021.

Haggart, Craig, *The demographic impact of the Civil wars on Scotland, Scotland 1567-1707*, University of Glasgow, 2018.

Haggart, Craig, T*he Engagement; Theocracy; the last Anglo-Scots war; and the Commonwealth: Scotland 1648-60, Scotland 1567-1707*, University of Glasgow, 2018.

Haggart, Craig, *The late medieval Church; the rise of Protestantism and Catholic reform, Scotland under the Stewart kings 1371 - 1603,* University of Glasgow, 2015.

Hall, Derek, *Scottish Monastic Landscapes*, Stroud, 2006.

Hankins, N. P. & Strawhorn, J. (Editors), *The Correspondence of James Boswell with James Bruce and Andrew Gibb, Overseers of the Auchinleck Estate*, Edinburgh, 1998.

Hay, John, *A Short History of Kilwinning Parish*, Kilwinning, 1988.

Houston, R. A. & White I. D., *Scottish Society 1500-1800*, Cambridge, 2005.

Index to Particular Register of sasines for Sheriffdom of Ayr and Bailiaries of Kyle, Carrick and Cunningham 1635-1660, Vol.II, Carnegie Library, Ayr.

Innes, Cosmo (editor), *Liber Sancte Marie de Melros*, Vol.1, Bannatyne Club, Edinburgh, 1837, Nos. 66-73, p55-64.

Knox, John, *History of the Reformation*, Edinburgh, 1949.

Livingstone, Matthew, *Register of the Privy Seal of Scotland/ Registrum secreti sigilli regnum Scotorum*, Vol.4, Edinburgh, 1908.

Love, Dane, *The History of Auchinleck; Village and Parish*, Auchinleck, 2015.

Love, Dane, *The River Ayr Way*, Auchinleck, 2006.

Meikle, Maureen M., *A British Frontier? Lairds and Gentlemen in the Eastern Borders, 1540-1603*, East Linton, 2004.

Morton, A. J., *An Independent Review of the History and Surface Archaeology of a forgotten Medieval Estate*, PE1209/D.

Mure, Sir William, Knight of Rowallan, *The History and Descent of the House of Rowallan Written Prior to 1657*, Glasgow, 1825.

National Records of Scotland.

Paterson, James, *History of the County of Ayr: with a Genealogical Account of the Families of Ayrshire*, 2 Vols., Edinburgh, 1847-52.

Paton, Henry (Editor), *The Clan Campbell Abstracts, Vol.V, Entries relating to Campbells in the early unprinted records relating to Ayrshire 1515 - 1650,* Edinburgh, 1913-22.

Pitcairn, Robert, *Ancient Criminal Trials in Scotland,* Vol.3, Edinburgh, 1833.

Retours of Services of Heirs 1544-1699 Inquisitionem ad capellam domini regis retornatarum abbreviatio Inquisitiones Generales

Robertson, George, *A Genealogical Account of the Principal Families in Ayrshire,* Vol.2, Irvine, 1824.

Rollie, James, *The Invasion of Ayrshire; a background to the county families,* Blanefield, 1980.

Romanes, Charles S. (Editor), *Selections from the records of the Regality of Melrose,* Edinburgh, 1915.

Sanderson, M. H. B., A*yrshire and the Reformation,* East Linton, 1997.

Sanderson, M. H. B., T*he Mauchline Account Book of Melrose Abbey 1527 - 1528,* AANHS, 2nd series, xi, 1976.

Sanderson, M. H. B., *Scottish Rural Society in the Sixteenth Century,* Edinburgh, 1982.

Scott, Hew, *Fasti Ecclesiae Scoticanae; The Succession of Ministers in the Church of Scotland from the Reformation,*

Vol.3, Synod of Glasgow and Ayr.

Shaw, John, *The Dalrymples of Langlands*, Bath, n.d.

Shearer, Joseph D., *Ayr and its People*, 2004.

Steven, Helen J., *Sorn Parish: Its History and Associations*, Kilmarnock, 1898.

Stewart, Dugald, *The Collected Works of Dugald Stewart*, Vol X, Edinburgh, 1858.

Taylor, Simon, *Ayrshire Place-Names: a rich seam still to mine*, Ayrshire Notes, 38, Autumn 2009.

Thomson, John Maitland, *The Register of the Great Seal of Scotland*, Vols. 6, 7 and 9, Edinburgh, 1892.

Yale University, Beinecke Rare Book and Manuscript Library, Boswell Collection GEN MSS 89 Series XV

Websites

Ayrshire History:
www.ayrshirehistory.com

Battlefield Trust:
www.battlefieldtrust.com

Battle of Linlithgow Bridge:

www.bolb.org.uk

British History Online:
british-history.ac.uk/glasgow-charters/1175-1649/no1

Cracroft's Peerage:
www.cracroftspeerage.co.uk

Dictionary of Scots Language:
www.dsl.ac.uk

Findmypast:
www.findmypast.co.uk

Jardine's Book of Martyrs:
drmarkjardine.wordpress.com

Meehan, Paula 'Museum':
poetryireland.ie

Milliken Genealogy:
Freepages.rootsweb.com/alanmilliken/genealogy/Research/ScottishRecords/Ayrshire/Mauchline.html

National Library of Scotland:
www.maps.nls.uk

Oxford Dictionary of National Biography:
www.oxforddnb.com

People of Medieval Scotland:

www.poms.ac.uk

Records of the Parliament of Scotland:
www.rps.ac.uk

Scottish Archive Network:
www.scan.org.uk

Scottish Covenanter Memorials Association:
www.covenanter.org.uk

ScotlandsPeople:
www.scotlandspeople.gov.uk

South Ayrshire Council:
southayrshirehistory.wordpress.com/page/7/

University of Glasgow Archives & Special Collections:
gla.ac.uk/myglasgow/archivespecialcollections

Photo Credits

Cover: Drumfork Fields and Fawsyde Castle. Andrew McInnes
Mungo Reid's (4) signature. Boswell Collection, General Collection, Beinecke Rare Book and Manuscript Library
Fig. 1: Heather House. Ordnance Survey Ayrshire Sheet XXIX survey 1856 publication date 1860. Reproduced with the permission of the National Library of Scotland
Fig. 2: Fermtouns at Drumfork. National Grid Maps 1940s – 1970s. Reproduced with the permission of the National Library of Scotland
Fig. 3: Blaeu Coila Provincia 1654. Reproduced with the permission of the National Library of Scotland
Fig. 4: Roy Military Survey of Scotland 1747 – 1755. Reproduced with the permission of the National Library of Scotland
Fig. 5: Mauchline Castle. Andrew McInnes
Fig. 6: Linlithgow Palace. From a painting of Andrew Spratt used with permission
Fig. 7: Repair after the siege of Tantallon Castle, 1528. From a painting of Andrew Spratt used with permission
Fig. 8: Thomas Hamilton's signature. Boswell Collection. General Collection, Beinecke Rare Book and Manuscript Library
Fig. 9: Clerk's practise page. Crown copyright. Data supplied by National Records of Scotland
Fig. 10: Mause Crawford's Testament. Crown copyright. Data supplied by National Records of Scotland
Fig. 11: Hills from Drumfork. Andrew McInnes

Fig.12: Ovir Logan sasine, 1606. Crown copyright. Data supplied by National Records of Scotland
Fig. 13: Brackenhill. Andrew McInnes
Fig. 14: Old Place of Auchinleck. Andrew McInnes
Fig. 15: Old Place of Auchinleck. Andrew McInnes
Fig. 16: Rainbow over Drumfork. Andrew McInnes
Fig. 17: Disposition of Brackenhill, 1648. Boswell Collection. General Collection, Beinecke Rare Book and Manuscript Library
Fig. 18: Auchinleck Kirk. Andrew McInnes
Fig. 19: Sorn Kirk. Andrew McInnes
Fig. 20: Special Retour for Margaret Dalrymple, 1688. Boswell Collection. General Collection, Beinecke Rare Book and Manuscript Library
Fig. 21: Nether Catrine House. With permission of Kenny Baird
Fig. 22: Tack of Hern alias Ballangape of Drumfork, 1710. Boswell Collection. General Collection, Beinecke Rare Book and Manuscript Library

Index

Illustrations are in bold.

***

INDEX PEOPLE

***

INDEX PLACES

The Lands of Drumfork